THE ECOLOGICAL PERSON

DISCLOSING NATURE AS THOU

LUK BOUCKAERT

YUNUS PUBLISHING

CONTENTS

In his book on 'eco-personalism' Luk Bouckaert makes a compelling case for renewing Personalist philosophy in the context of the current ecological, social, and ethical crisis. He suggests that the classical form of personalism represented by Jacques Maritain, Emmanuel Mounier and others does not work in the era of the Anthropocene characterized by climate change, biodiversity loss, ecosystem collapse, welfare malaises, and global inequalities. The ecological extension and reinterpretation of the concept of the person requires new answers to the question "What does it mean to be human?" The central problem of Luk Bouckaert's book is how to reconcile ecological thinking and personalism.

Bouckaert argues that we must change our relationship with our planet and this requires the restoration of the spiritual bond with nature. The book develops a philosophical position that takes the personal responsibility towards the other seriously and does justice to nature as a source for creation of meaning. Bouckaert suggests that we must experience our relationship with nature in face-to-face, personalized forms, something as the 'I-Thou' relationship described by Martin Buber. In this way our encounter with plants, animals and other things of nature can be deeply personal and generate meaningful interactions.

As a basis for his eco-personalism Bouckaert uses Albert Schweitzer's eco-philosophical principle of reverence for life ("Ehrfurcht vor dem Leben"). Although Schweitzer was a Christian theologian, his principle of reverence for life is compatible with Hindu philosophy. The famous formulation of his principle "I am life that wants to live, in the midst of life that wants to live" can be a quote from a Vedantic text too. Modern biological research also supports Schweitzer eco-philosophy. The so-called Santiago theory developed by Humberto Maturana and Francisco Varela discovered that living organisms are self-making ("autopoietic") systems which follow their own "telos" in creating and maintaining themselves in interaction with their environment. So the concept of wellbeing or flourishing is applicable not only for human beings but also for non-human beings.

Eco-personalism presents a new hope for integrating humanism and ecology on the ground of spirituality. Luk Bouckaert's book is a welcome contribution to philosophy which can induce progressive changes in social practices in many fields of life. "Tolle, lege" ("take up and read") as Augustine said.

Laszlo Zsolnai

Corvinus University of Budapest

European SPES Institute – Leuven

Blackfriars Hall, University of Oxford

L'histoire est notre maître.
(E.Mounier)

INTRODUCTION

Change often follows crisis. In the absence of crisis, those who have little to gain by change have no incentive to transcend their short-term self-interest. But an imminent crisis forces to act. The Corona pandemic, for example, made us rapidly switch to previously unthinkable behavior. However once the immediate threat is gone, the pressure to return to business as usual is great. I suspect that the pandemic only was an interruption of our normal life habits, not a fundamental change.

The climate crisis and its slow and irreversible threat is different. When exactly the tipping point will occur, we do not know, but we are gradually crossing critical thresholds. More and more regions are hit by drought, famine, forest fires, storms, or floods. Is this the beginning of the end of the 'Anthropocene Era'? Nobody knows. What is clear is that the many years of overexploiting our planetary resources are turning that very planet against us. Scientific reports and climate protests, spearheaded by our younger generations, have not yet been translated into a global, adequate, political action. The International 'free-rider' and 'my country first' mentality undermine the sense of global responsibility. Could more be done? If the pressure placed on governments and institutions by citizens continues to increase, most certainly, but this means that we must all ask ourselves whether we are personally prepared to pay the price to reverse the global warming curve.

This essay hopes to contribute to that necessary self-examination, but a quest never starts in a vacuum. My own search began as a student of philosophy at Leuven during the 'golden sixties' when I read the works of some French authors of Personalistic philosophy (J. Maritain, E. Mounier, E. Levinas, P. Ricoeur). Their personalist focus on reciprocal social responsibility was translated by the Christian Democrats into a political ideology promoting the idea of a socially corrected market economy, called the 'Rhineland model.' Rhineland Personalism gave postwar Europe a strong political and economic boost towards rebuilding itself. Can a revised version of the same principles be used to tackle the climate crisis? Or do we need a more radical shift?

This essay is not a blueprint for political action. It is an attempt to re-evaluate the philosophical foundations of Personalism and its implications for our self-perception, our views of the future, and our dealings with nature. I start with two research questions. The first question concerns our self-perception as a person. Is it possible for a Personalist, who values the unique dignity of every person, to subordinate their freedom to nature as an eco-system? Can nature be more to the human than an object of scientific analysis, a reservoir of raw materials, a space to travel in, or a background for beauty and romance? The second question is perhaps even more challenging. Today the word 'hope' appears in many writings and speeches, but what do we mean by hope? Can it with-stand the scientific scenarios predicting climate catastrophe?

Thirty years ago Geert Bouckaert and I wrote the book,

Metafysiek en Engagement. (*Metaphysics and Engagement: A Personalist Vision of Community and Economy*, Leuven, 1992.) We were interested in the relevance, or lack thereof, of Personalism in the then current societal debate in which the 'Communitarians' had the upper hand over both right-wing (neo-liberal) and left-wing (egalitarian) versions of individualism. Social bonding was the new focus promoted by Communitarians. Neo-liberal globalization had upset the balance between autonomy and social bonding, market and government. This disturbed balance called for a critical reflection. While communitarians emphasized a return to traditional values and virtues, the personalist position highlighted the need of social responsibility and spiritually driven entrepreneurship.

Today, the challenge is far more important. The survival of future generations and of the planet is at stake. In such a context discussions on autonomy and tradition become less relevant. We need a paradigm shift that critically revises our self-perception in relation to nature. In trying to envisage this paradigm shift, this essay draws much of its inspiration from authors who formulated already this ecological shift around a hundred years ago, during or just after the First World War. Albert Schweitzer wrote his *Culture and Ethics* as a German prisoner of war in a French labor camp. Teilhard de Chardin compiled his *Hymn to Matter* at the front, while serving as a stretcher bearer. Mahatma Gandhi began his *Experiments with Truth* in India in 1914 and Martin Buber published *I and Thou* in 1923. I regard these thinkers (and doers) as pioneers of eco-personalism. So, I was pleasantly surprised to find that eco-personalism disclosed itself *before* the better known French movement of social personalism inspired by J. Maritain and E. Mounier, which was a response to the inter-bellum crisis of the 1930s.

My own interest in personalism is linked to the story of SPES, a network that started in 2000 as a small and informal 'Study-group for Personalistic Economics and Society' (abbreviated to SPES). Later, SPES grew into an acronym for 'Spirituality in Economics and Society.' From a local group of friends it developed into an international network for spiritual revitalization. Professor Laszlo Zsolnai, co-founder and president of The European SPES Institute, introduced a Buddhist-inspired focus on deep ecology. This has now come full circle for me. Personalism, spirituality, and ecology come together in the old but revived tradition of eco-personalism.

An essay is a thought-experiment. An experiment with truth, as Gandhi put it. Such an experiment does not take place in a laboratory, amidst controlled conditions. Truth is tested in the laboratory of our daily lives in a very different way. We test our reflected subjective experiences against each other and against those of other people. I thus hope this essay can contribute to a collective investigation into what it means to be a person today and to help us unlock the future together.

The essay integrates three previously published articles. I would like to thank the friends at the *U Turn project* of UCSIA, the *Trends Chair in Economics of Hope* (University of Antwerpen), and the *Tijdschrift voor Geestelijk Leven* for giving me full support to revise and to republish these articles. But my warmest thanks goes to Henri Ghesquiere, who launched the idea of an English translation of the Dutch *Ecopersonalisme*; to Sabine Denis, who took up the challenge and carefully translated the original Dutch text; and to Mikael Bouckaert, who re-edited the manuscript. Without them there would be no English version of this essay.

CHAPTER 1

BEYOND THE RHINELAND MODEL

Humans at the centre was the title of a UCSIA webinar on European values that took place on 7 October, 2020. This title excellently reflects the focus of personalism on the dignity of every human being and its deep resistance to the oppression of human freedom and responsibility by the arrogance of systems, be it ideological, economic, political, or religious systems. But today the title raises questions. It seems to imply an anthropocentrism that puts humans above nature, a belief that in the long run leads us to alienation from nature and overexploitation of natural resources. Shouldn't we be putting nature ahead of people? Many today argue for radical eco-centric thinking as an alternative to harmful anthropocentrism. In this essay I explore whether we can reconcile eco-centric and personalistic thinking; and, if so, how?

Personalism in the post-war period stands for a political ideology that in its more practical application is called the 'Rhineland model.' This model promotes a social market economy with a firm commitment to economic growth, and coupled to a fair redistribution of income, high consumption, unrestrained use of fossil fuels and non-renewable raw materials. It continues to contribute to the economic plundering of our planet and to pave the way to an increasingly visible and dire climate catastrophe.

Hence, if personalism is to regain its critical and revolutionary power within the context of today, it must make a radical U-turn.[1] Such a shift would entail a critical investigation of the presuppositions of the Rhineland model, and, where necessary, moving beyond it. Only in this way can a transition take place from a growth economy to a sustainable life economy (which this essay will refer to as 'the economy of hope'). This transition will allow for change in both our self-perception and in our view and relationship to nature.

RHINELAND PERSONALISM

Personalism as a philosophical and political theory originated in the crisis of the 1930s. This crisis came amidst the erosion of parliamentary democracy in Western countries, the rise of fascism, the stock market crash, high unemployment, and disturbing suicide rates. In short, a context of deep social and economic malaise, which eventually unleashed itself in the Second World War and its sixty million victims.

What were the roots of this societal wave of frustration, impotence, opportunism, and self-glorification? It was more than just a political and economic crisis. Personalists initially interpreted the events as symptoms of a crisis of civilization. The classical metaphysics in which man was positioned within a God-ordered hierarchy and world had eroded. The modern alternative, the Cartesian worldview of the autonomous man conquering the world and directing its progress, was in turn questioned by Sigmund Freud, Karl Marx, Friedrich Nietzsche, and other maverick thinkers. Personalism, or rather the various groups of personalists, all shared this conviction in a deep crisis of civilization. Opinions differed as to the solution.

It is important to emphasize this diversity. There never was a singular Personalism, rather, a great variety. Jacques Maritain created a neo-Thomistic Personalism and his vision has strongly shaped the political ideology of Christian Democracy. Emmanuel Mounier and the movement around his *Esprit* magazine was inspired by the radical existential philosophy of Sören Kierkegaard. Mounier and Kierkegaard were both anti-system thinkers, sharply critical of all forms of centralized power that undermines personal creativity and responsibility. Finally, in the 1930s, a fringe Personalist school, led by Bernard Charbonneau and Jacques Ellul, emerged that did center itself around ecological themes. In a 1937 manifesto entitled *Le sentiment de la Nature, force révolutionnaire*, these authors formulated a fierce critique of technocracy and the dominance of instrumental thinking (Roy 1999).

Rhineland Personalism distilled from these divergent philosophical ideas a political ideology that served as the backbone for Christian Democracy in post-war Europe. The starting point is the human individual as a combination of individual freedom and social interdependence. Christian Democracy likes to present itself as the party of the center, a 'third way' between the individual and the collective, between the market and the government, between the left and the right, between liberalism and socialism. But the center is not an empty space. It is a dynamic place where civil society acquires a political voice—through trade unions, health and family care institutions, representative organisations for education and the whole network of communities of civil life. The Christian Democratic vision balances between the left and the right. In the 1980s, under the pressure of globalization, neoliberal market thinking became dominant. Today growing inequality, the climate crisis, and the Corona pandemic have put the government back in the drivers seat. In these circumstances, can a centrist political philosophy provide an adequate answer to the ecological challenge?

Emmanuel Mounier, one of the founders of personalism, wrote a sentence during the crisis of the 1930s that still resonates with me: "Our crisis is both an economic and a spiritual crisis, a crisis of structures and a crisis of man. We must go beyond the statement by the poet Péguy: The Revolution will be ethical or it will not be. I claim: The ethical revolution will be economic or it will not be." (Mounier 1962: 183) The young Mounier and his colleagues around *Esprit* were convinced that only a 'spiritual revolution' could provide an answer to the crisis of their time. The insight that the economy plays a central role in this process of spiritual renaissance is surprising because it relates Mounier to Marx. Either radical change will take root in the socio-economic fabric or nothing will essentially change.

WHO AM I? BACK TO THE HUMAN PERSON

I consider Personalism to be a dialogical philosophy that aims at transforming the individual into a person. Often the modern concept of the person is reduced to that of an individual claiming its autonomy and the protection of its rights. But in the personalist tradition the person refers to a relational subject characterised by its deep interdependence and connection with all that is. In other words: there is distinction between the person as an ego-self and the person as inter-self. The inter-self refers both to the actual connection of people with each other and to their ethical responsibility for each other. The latter transforms an individual into a genuine person.

A person cannot be reduced to some general characteristic, for example, as an abstract being with universal rights and duties. A person can never be fully grasped in such descriptive concepts. Becoming a genuine person is first and foremost a subjective process in which I become aware of my own complex relationship with reality through dialogue with others and, at the same time, of the fact that I myself must shape this complexity.

The core idea of existential personalism is not the abstract question, 'what is a person' but, rather, 'who am *I* as a person? What is *my* calling and purpose?' Only I-in-relation-to-the-other, and no one else, can answer that question, and I can only answer it with how I live my life. Sören Kierkegaard (1813-1855) characterizes personhood as "a relationship that relates to itself." (Kierkegaard 1983) This somewhat cryptic expression gestures towards the fact that becoming a person does not only refer to the system of relations in which I am woven. Beyond the system there is a transcendent self that perceives this complexity. We never coincide absolutely with our relationships. This makes possible a transformation of life as a given fact into life as a personal responsibility. Although we cannot change the circumstances we have been thrown into, we can regulate our way of coping with the facts of life. As a dependent being I cannot change the world, but I can choose to act bravely and honorably when faced with our contemporary world's own challenges and corruptions. For Kierkegaard, individuals only become persons when they freely *choose* to live a responsible life. That is to say, responsible for their existence as part of the whole. No one is born a person. Prior to the ethical choice, there is only a 'capacity' of living a responsible and connected life.

Person is etymologically derived from *persona* (stage mask). Actors in antiquity often wore masks to heighten their voice and to give their character more expression. So too the existential meaning of the person: by publicly giving voice and expression to my responsibility as an individual, I become a person. The latin *persona* is also closely related to *prophet*, a combination of the Greek word *phèmi*, or speaking, and *pro*, or forward. A person thinks, speaks, and acts pro-phetically—the utterance or act opens up, creates, the future. Without knowing what the future holds I am nonetheless called upon to give it a meaning and purpose and to take responsibility for it.

For the guidance of social action a philosophical framework and a political ideology are essential, but the existential element of Personalism, often neglected because it is considered too subjective, is even more so. Awareness of one's own subjective truth and calling has to come first. Anyone who turns the matter around and equates Personalism primarily with a theory or an ideology misses the point of living personalism. The first item on a Personalist's agenda is a personal spiritual resourcing.

When Mahatma Gandhi took over the leadership of the independence movement in India he reserved a day a week for himself—*because* of his considerable responsibility—to fast and to nourish his spirituality. When we founded SPES twenty years ago as a network for the spiritual resourcing of Personalism, we did so with the conviction that without that re-sourcing Personalism would evaporate.

Many questions remain unanswered. Where does this call for responsibility come from? Is it nature itself that prompts us? Or is it the vulnerable other who awakens in me the sense of responsibility? Or a divine source that inspires me? Or a connection between all these elements? Let us first focus on the question of how the subjective process of becoming a person relates us to nature. From there answers to these other unanswered questions might also start to emerge.

FROM EGO TO ECO

The fact that we are employing all our knowledge and resources to destroying nature makes painfully obvious the conclusion that we must change our relationship to our planet. Some believe Green Capitalism to be the answer: a smart economy based on new technologies that produce more goods more sustainably. But can this answer repair our existential and spiritual alienation from nature, or does it merely exploit nature more efficiently? The Deep Ecology movement thinks the answer lies elsewhere, in the restoration of the spiritual bond with nature. Humans form a part of nature and receive from her their zest of life—an idea that can be found in many old spiritual traditions, such as the Ubuntu philosophy in parts of Africa and the Mother Earth spirituality of some Native American tribes.

The Indian-British activist Satish Kumar defines spirituality as the transition from ego to eco. (*You Are, Therefore I Am. A Declaration of Dependence,* 2002.) There is only a change of one letter between the two terms, but the experience of the self they refer to is totally different. Whereas the ego-self is the center of the world, the eco-self is part of an infinite whole. It receives its identity from the greater whole of creation:

> The Hindus use the saying 'So Hum'—'You are, therefore I am.' Like you, I did not fall from heaven: I was born of a mother. My mother is, therefore I am. I have learnt a lot from Buddha, from Mahavira, from Jesus, from Mohamed.

These great masters are, therefore I am. I feed on the fruits of the earth, the sun gives me warmth, the water quenches my thirst, the air fills my lungs. These elements are, therefore I am. I have found much inspiration in the works of Gandhi, of Tolstoy, of Tagore, of Van Gogh. My ancestors are, therefore I am (Kumar, 2002).

It is remarkable that Kumar and many other deep ecologists describe the eco-experience exclusively in positive forms of inter-dependence and receptivity. The human being feels connected to a harmonious nature and to the wisdom of good leaders. But what about our negative experiences of nature, our suffering at the hands of evil leaders? Can one also say, "The tsunami is, therefore I am"? "Hitler is, therefore I am"? I think that the eco-centric view of nature ignores the confrontation with evil and death. It is often too romantic.

How can the natural environment be a source of meaning in a world wherein conflict and destruction often dominate? In my view, Albert Schweitzer's eco-thinking offers a valid answer to that question. Initially, there seems little difference between an eco-centrist like Satish Kumar and an eco-personalist like Schweitzer. Both describe how the person is born from a great receptivity to the life given to us by nature. But there is a crucial difference in their understandings and experiences of nature.

Albert Schweitzer is best known as the white doctor who founded a hospital village in Lambarene, Gabon. He was awarded the Nobel Peace Prize for doing so. Much less well known is how he sought a new foundation for Western ethics in the African jungle. (Schweitzer, 1983) He started writing down his new ethics when, as Germans living in Gabon during the First World War, he and his wife were placed under house arrest by French soldiers and later transferred to

European prison camps. For him, the violence of the war was further proof of the bankruptcy of Western academic philosophy. His vision is strongly related to Mahatma Gandhi's ethic of nonviolence and to Franciscan ecology. He was inspired by Lev Tolstoy and by Johann Wolfgang Goethe's nature mysticism.

In his autobiography, Schweitzer tells of how a lifelong search led to his discovery of his foundational ethical principle in Africa. (Schweitzer, 1998) During a three-day boat trip on the Ogowe River to visit a sick patient he had an intense spiritual experience. In the waning light of sunset he was passing a group of hippos when the words *"Ehrfurcht vor dem Leben"* ("Reverence for life") suddenly came to him. Later he would sum up this experience in the phrase:

I am life that wants to live,
in the midst of life that wants to live.

Ehrfurcht is difficult to translate. The word expresses an attitude of awe (Furcht) and honour (Ehr). Schweitzer believed that respect for life begins with a reflexive awareness of one's own will to live: 'I am life that wants to live' while Descartes starts from the self as a thinking being. For Schweitzer thinking is only one of the forms in which the will to live expresses itself. In this Schweitzer was inspired by A. Schopenhauer and F. Nietzsche, both of whom took the individual's will to live as the starting point for their philosophies. But Schweitzer adds something new. *My* experience of life is one of solidarity: *all* life desires to live, each in its own way. People and animals, flowers and stars, the earth and the cosmos, everything that is and lives, is connected to each other by the shared will to live. Because of this shared zest, nature is not a means in the service of man. The Kantian categorical imperative does not apply to human beings solely. Everything that lives has its own authentic meaning that we must recognize and respect. Reverence for life finally connects us to the Source of Life. In recognizing the diversity of life forms, Life is implicitly honored as the inexhaustible Source of new life forms. "By becoming aware of the solidarity with all beings and putting this solidarity into practice, we come, and this is the only way, to a true communion with the infinite Being to which all beings belong." (Schweitzer, 2004: 256)

Schweitzer was very radical in the application of his universal eco-principle. For example, he refuses to make a principled distinction between higher and lower forms of life. Every life, from 'high' to 'low,' has within it an intrinsic value and beauty and thus deserves the same respect. It makes no difference whether it is a spider, a hippopotamus, a flower, or a human being. Anyone who establishes a hierarchy by that very act ends up exploiting and destroying the supposedly lower forms of life. It is only in immediate, lived situations that we must make unavoidable choices based on contextual discernment and consideration, and place one form of life above another. This means that human beings are not automatically given priority. In his youth, Schweitzer supported the emerging animal protection movement. He joined the protests against bullfighting, animals test, and even opposed the picking of flowers to put them in vases. From childhood onwards he had a scrupulous fear of hurting animals. Schweitzer, with his universal eco-principle of respect for life, is one of the fathers of deep ecology. His commitment as a doctor was a fundamental part of this.

The difficult point in any nature philosophy is the ambiguous nature of nature. Many deep ecologists fall back upon a dichotomy wherein nature represents harmony and balance, and humanity embodies disruption and exploitation.

But this overestimates the bad in humanity and the good in nature. Nature is also Janus-faced. It is as much the source of beauty, cohesion, and goodness, as it is of destruction, brutal competition, 'survival of the fittest,' and so on. Despite solidarity and altruism among animals and systems of cooperation in nature, there is also an abundance of cruel competition. One human's loss is another human's gain—so too in the animal kingdom. Schweitzer knew this from life, not books. He was a doctor who found himself forced to kill viruses and bacteria in order to cure people. When there were too many cats roaming around the village, Schweitzer decided to stop their proliferation.

Schweitzer believed that the ethical norm of 'respect for nature and for all beings' cannot simply be derived from nature itself, wherein there exists no such law. In this sense Schweitzer is not an eco-centrist. Only when we experience ourselves as *moral,* not merely as *natural,* beings can we embrace the idea of unconditional respect for all life. Plants and animals do not suffer from this moral utopia. This is where humans differ from other life forms. But this does not mean that we can ascribe to ourselves a higher hierarchical status or reduce other creatures to objects of use. To do so, or not do so, is a moral choice, with serious consequences. Schweitzer believes we become a person at the moment we make the *choice* of respect for life. At that moment we are most deeply ourselves and most connected to all living beings and to the source of life. The objectification and misuse of nature, conversely, deprives us of our own experience of subjectivity—that is, of life.

We have seen how a new self-perception can lead to a new conception of nature and a spiritual experience of universal connectedness. The ego relates to itself as an eco-self. It finds in the undercurrent of consciousness an intuitive point of experience where it is connected to all of creation. The Song of the Sun by St Francis gives this basic experience of the eco-self a moving, poetic expression.

THE SOCIO-ECONOMIC CONSEQUENCES

The moral and spiritual law of reverence for life is a call to transform nature and the human being from chaos to order, from destruction to harmony. Every person has to fight evil and negativity in their own habitat. They must take care of the whole of creation in their own place and establish an 'economy of hope.'

An economy of hope breathes with two lungs: the rational lung of sustainable efficiency and the spiritual lung of respect for life. After all, sustainability can be achieved from two very different angles. It can be implemented from the mainstream economic logic that only breathes with the rational lung. This leads, at best, to an eco-corrected market economy that amounts to green capitalism. There may be a pursuit of long-term efficiency that mitigates the negative effects of the economy, but the underlying logic of economic growth remains unchanged. Even if economic growth creates employment for many people and offers opportunities for social redistribution of wealth, it logically leads to the over-exploitation of the planet.

The only sustainable remedy is to learn to breathe with two lungs. The challenge is to develop an economic logic in which nature is treated as a value in itself, not as a means. That is why we speak of an economy of life rather than of an economy of growth. The focus on life as a source of material and spiritual wealth opens a much wider perspective than the focus on GDP. It also requires more discernment and consideration of values. We still have a long way to go. New technology and respect for life seem far from finding one another. Mahatma Gandhi with his spinning wheel 'economy of self-sufficiency' (swadeshi); Ivan Ilyich with his plea for 'convivial technology'; and Ernst Friedrich Schumacher with his commitment to 'intermediate technology' have been experimental pioneers in this field.

A fine contemporary example of this combination of efficiency and respect is the work of German architect Thomas Rau, who was recently a guest at Etion Forum, 2020. The German architect feels that the current progress in the field of sustainability is towards optimizing the current system rather than fundamentally changing it: "We are using our raw materials more efficiently and sparingly, but the system remains the same. In the end, we throw the raw materials away. That's why we have to question the whole system and opt for circularity." (Cobbaut, 2020)

In a fully circular economy, raw materials are not exhausted, but used permanently. How is that possible? Through innovation. An example that Rau himself uses is the addition to each building of a materials passport, listing the materials used in the construction. The architects then know exactly which and how many materials are in the building, when maintenance is required, and how they can disassemble them. The materials are registered on an online public platform and can be reused endlessly. The building retains a certain financial value. Houses are never completely written off. Their materials remain available for future products. This incentivizes manufacturers to opt for better design and material choices.

CONCLUSION

Respect for life is a powerful and unifying eco-concept. It unlocks the solidarity of life and the intrinsic dignity of all living beings. Schweitzer's example shows how this eco-postulate finds its origin in the moral and spiritual consciousness of the person. The anchoring of the eco-concept in the person as a spiritual and moral being makes Schweitzer a personalist. He is also a profoundly ecological thinker who does not link our human capacity for moral thinking to human superiority over nature. It is this hierarchical thinking that leads us, consciously or unconsciously, to the abuse of nature. Schweitzer's eco-philosophy attempts to correct this misconception by giving man and nature a shared basis of solidarity in the will to live. He rejects anthropocentrism, while avoiding the romanticism of eco-centrism. He accomplishes the U-turn towards an authentic eco-personalism.

CHAPTER 2

THE POWER OF HOPE

An 'economy of hope' is often interpreted as a 'correction' of the prevailing economic system. Sustainability then turns out to be no more than the manifesto of green capitalism—growth in technology will lead to less pollution, greater consumption will lead to higher rates of employment. More electric cars, more cattle and chickens in low-emission sheds, more travel in less polluting airplanes. The return on capital and investment remains the driving force of the system. An economy of exploitation is corrected but in no way replaced: greenhouse gas emissions, burn-out, depression, and inequality continue to increase; biodiversity and natural resources continue to decline; the power of multinational corporations remains unchallenged. Why are our corrections to the economy so insufficient? What are the blind spots in the system? Can't the government take more radical measures against the lobby groups without endangering jobs?

AN ECONOMY WITHOUT HOPE

Advocating an economy of hope may appeal to idealists but to realists it sounds soft. No one is against hope, of course, but everyone interprets it differently. Happiness is also something different to everyone. Misery and despair, the opposites of happiness and hope, are far more universally recognized and easily identifiable. Let us therefore start with the reverse image of an economy of hope: an economy without hope. Nobody wants it, but we are moving in that direction.

An economy without hope is an economy that makes its own future impossible. It is an economy that strives for short-term gain while destroying itself in the long run. Analogous to an auto-immune disease—when one's own defense system will attack its healthy cells—the logic of pragmatism and efficiency can destroy a healthy community. Such a self-destructive economy could also be described as a *predatory economy*.

Many of the symptoms of the predatory economy are familiar. They are scientifically documented in the report of the Club of Rome in 1972 and the reports of the International Climate Panel of the United Nations. The main cause is the overexploitation of the earth driven by the perceived need to increase the GDP of countries and regions. Growth is believed to be the necessary condition for the repayment of debts, material prosperity, higher employment, and the financing of social security. Growth is the god of economics, universally worshipped: a country like China is doing well because it is growing; Japan is doing poorly because it is too flat or stagnant. Growth is also thought necessary for political stability. And so the circle is made complete. We destroy the earth to save ourselves, which leads to the opposite: we destroy ourselves.

Ecological overexploitation is not the only problem. The psychological symptoms of social abuse—burn-out, depression, suicide—are equally alarming. Medical remedies can contain or camouflage them, but they cannot uproot the socio-economic mechanisms from which these symptoms arise. In our current labor market, higher wages have to be compensated by higher labor productivity, which in practice means doing more with less people and dismissing those who are less skilled. Even the most favorable social system cannot prevent dismissed people from feeling useless, and from suffering psychologically and mentally from what Kierkegaard calls the 'fatal disease of despair.' Out of social concern government and trade unions attempt to reduce the work-pressure, but this results in higher costs and a loss of competitiveness, which in turn increases the pressure to replace socially oriented business leaders by capitalists more willing to exploit the worker.

This is the flaw of an economy without hope: people lose their soul and joy of life. The *homo economicus* is no longer an industrious and moral person as Adam Smith envisaged him. He is degraded to a greedy monster, an unrelenting capitalist, or a never satisfied consumer. So long as the system within which this being must operate is driven by the logic of maximum return on capital and labour, so too will the human being in its mode remain the same unrelenting and never satisfied *homo economicus*. But who can change the system? Do we have to wait in anxious anticipation for a savior that never will come?

A crucial step to overcome the deadly drive of the system is to realise that the relentless *homo economicus* who wants to achieve as many goals as possible and to exploit the scarce resources as much as possible is not outside but within us. His way of thinking in terms of maximum efficiency is part of our own mind. This does not mean that we as economic maximisers of our ambitions and goals are always egoistic and greedy. The logic of maximum efficiency and productivity is not incommensurate with the achievement of social goals. Whether we are social entrepreneurs, hospital managers, school headmasters, dockworkers, handymen, investment fund managers, welfare ministers, or green party members, we must act efficiently and productively to survive and grow—so goes the thinking of *homo economicus*.

And it would be an illusion and even an impoverishment to banish this efficiency thinking. The problem however is that it has become so dominant that we no longer know how to think and act otherwise. Our consciousness has shrunk to a kind of calculating intelligence guided by the logic of optimization. The first Industrial Revolution had replaced muscles with machines to make us more productive; the digital revolution will replace our intelligence by robots of all kinds in order to support our desire to be more efficient. Those who do not participate in this process will lose their position in the competitive marketplace. Under the pressure of increased efficiency and productivity, our consciousness will be colonized because, in short, our creations are capable of higher levels of efficiency than their creators.

THE LEVERAGE OF HOPE

I read somewhere that hope is like a weed. It always reappears, no matter how much we try to remove it. As an antidote for our fear of the future, it always grows up as a kind of optimistic illusion. In the corona period, for example, the news cycle rapidly oscillated back and forth between optimistic and pessimistic predictions and expectations. But let us not concentrate on hope as a superficial weed but rather on the power of hope as a life-giving plant.

In periods of crisis hope is an indispensable but difficult *choice.* That choice requires a permanent reflection on different kinds of hope. If you listen carefully to the language you will notice how layered the idea of hope is. The French language, for example, makes a distinction between two levels of hope. The masculine *espoir* refers to the ego (derived from the French '*j'espère*'—I hope), which intervenes in the actual world and creates the future on the basis of its proactive imagination and calculation. *Espoir* is hope as project. It feeds on scientific forecasts, but also on our utopian projections of an ideal society. Hope is the confidence that we will achieve a positive outcome.

The other French word for hope is *espérance* (derived from the French *espérant*—hoping). Hope here refers to taking part in a process, to participation. We receive, rather than create, this variety of hope. It is a future that happens to us, not one of our making. The process presupposes a contemplative attitude, an openness to what is yet to come, and what is about to meet us. I have elsewhere called this *espérance* the meta-hope: hope beyond the makeable and imaginable. Hope as a spiritual force that transforms not only ourselves, but also the broader evolution and the cosmos *from within*. The future as a process of unfolding meaning.

These two forms of hope are easily recognizable in society. The socially engineered hope resonates strongly, for example, in Obama's, *yes we can,* and the later German echo in Merkel's, *wir schaffen das.* We can achieve whatever we strive for as long as all of us work together. Transposed to the climate crisis, this reads: if we persistently respect the rules and criteria that experts recommend on the basis of scientific prognoses, we will (re)enter the utopian realm of sustainable freedom. The future is ours to make. Trust and hope in society increase with the probability of the sought-for outcome. This phenomenon is corroborated in a recent study on hope in the Netherlands.[1] Reality, however, is often far less predictable and far more messy than we think. The world is not a boat in which some captain decides the correct destination and everyone else rows in that one direction. Hope in society often turns into disappointment, frustration, betrayal, and judgment.

Fortunately, there is a second dimension to hope, poetically described by Charles Péguy as *la petite fille espérance* (*the little girl hope*). *Espérance* presents an alternative to the utopia of a perfect society. It is founded on the conviction that history, despite all its misery, has a meaning, which will be revealed in due course, at the moment of Kairos. What we may ultimately expect is uncertain, but the *little girl hope*, like a GPS for the soul of humanity, will show us the way. Hope is the resilience to start all over again and to search for a way forward based on our inner and spiritual conviction that what we do is meaningful. Vaclaf Havel expressed it as follows: "Hope is an ability to work for something that is good, not just because it stands a chance to succeed. Hope is definitely not the same thing as optimism. It is not the conviction that something will turn out well, but the certainty that something makes sense, regardless of how it turns out." (Havel, 1990) Gandhi chose these words: "Our task is to work from our sense of what is just and right and to place the outcome in God's hands." Albert Camus puts the same idea of hope in the mouth of Tarrou, a rich and young traveler converted to a "holiness without God" who at the risk of his life decides to help people starving from the plague: "I only know that one must do what must be done ...; only this can give us hope of peace or, failing that, of a good death." (La Peste, 1947)

Nothing lifts the soul like hope, but let us remain critical. Is our faith in history as a meaningful process well founded? Marx believed that the inner contradictions of capitalism would lead to its own demise and, from its ashes, would rise a communal and classless society. The dreamers of the 'Third Reich' and the Islamic State, and, closer to home, the 'American Dream' place not only history but also God on their side. They draw from this the legitimacy to use violence. To what extent can *la petite fille espérance*, the meta-hope, be distinguished from these utopian and ideological projections of hope? The difference is that the utopian form of hope relies on a *concept* of an ideal society. There is a totalitarian side to this kind of utopia. Meta-hopefulness relies not on a concept but rather on a direct experience of the *vulnerability* of people and things. It requires a constant critical awareness to know whether our ideals and behavior are in line with this ethical sense of vulnerability or, rather, are driven by an ideological concept of hope. In the chapter on care as hope, we will elaborate on this experience of vulnerability.

Two forms of despair correspond to the two forms of hope. There is the despair we inflict on ourselves by pursuing wrong or contradictory goals. Despair in this case is the disappointment not to realise our intentions and ambitions. But there is a deeper despair that comes from the appropriation of hope as our property, thereby destroying the free gift of *espérance*. When hope is reduced into a thing we want to appropriate, it will lose its creative power and instead paralyse the soul. Despair, then, can lead to a complete loss of the sense of life. In *The Sickness Unto Death* (1848), Kierkegaard analyses this process step by step and concludes that despair is worse than death.

The great Russian writer Tolstoy knew this firsthand. He experienced an existential crisis of meaning at the height of his career and contemplated suicide. He overcame his despair by realizing that the serfs and peasants exploited on his own property, by him, still found a meaning in their miserable lives, through religion, while he, a rich aristocrat, no longer could. He converted, embarked upon an ascetic lifestyle (much to the annoyance of his wife), and defended the peasants against the Orthodox Church and other exploiters. Gandhi would call his second 'ashram' in South Africa, Tolstoy Farm, a peasant commune of non-violent resistance to British rule.

Tolstoy and Gandhi teach us that despair can only be turned around by allowing ourselves to be touched by the suffering and resilience of others. Real hope does not arise from thought. Hope begins, as Levinas tirelessly repeats, when we receive the future as a personal gift from *the hurting eyes of the Other*. Hope is to see in the suffering of the other (and, more broadly, of all creation) a way to a new future. True hope is not utopian, a dream of a perfect society born of abstraction. Martin Luther King's dream of racial harmony, for example, could be so boldly announced during the March on Washington because he had been suffering for and working towards it his entire life.

Gandhi and Tolstoy also teach us that economic pragmatism is an inadequate response to a deep crisis. Economic pragmatism is an attempt, in the name of realism, to correct the existing order and power relations in the interests of short- and/or long-term efficiency. The power of hope, on the other hand, lifts us out of our individual or collective ego position and opens up other perspectives that are impossible within the existing system. *Homo sperans*, the man/woman of hope, leaves room for the impossible and the unthinkable. A look at Gandhi's ideas on economic reform will make this clear.

GANDHI'S ECONOMY OF HOPE

Mohandas 'Mahatma' (great soul) Gandhi's story of resistance begins in South Africa, on his journey from Durban to Pretoria. He had finished his law studies in London but was unable to find a suitable job in India. His brother was able to secure him a South African commission from an Indian-owned company. After London (by no means an egalitarian society itself), the overt racism against Indians in South Africa horrified the young Gandhi. Indians were not allowed to travel first or second class on trains. Gandhi booked a first class train ticket. A passenger was disturbed by his presence and called the conductor. Gandhi stubbornly refused an order to move to third class. He was brutally removed from the train by guards in Maritzburg station. He spent that winter night in the station alone, with only his hand luggage and no coat. He realized that he was faced with a choice: fight for his rights or return to India. Gandhi decided to fight against injustice. The next day, thanks to his employer, he was able to travel by bus to Pretoria.

Fifty years later, Gandhi referred to this event as the start of his engagement in nonviolent resistance to the structural discrimination against Indians in South Africa. This resistance became the *Satyagraha* movement in 1906. Satyagraha means 'holding on to truth' or, one might say, 'standing up for truth.' Gandhi also defined it as "resisting untruth by truthful means." The fighters against injustice had to be prepared to suffer and even to die for the truth. Tolstoy Farm near Johannesburg became the centre of the Satyagraha movement and supported nonviolent resistance to any form of discrimination by the British occupiers. Tolstoy Farm was an ashram, a self-sufficient commune whose members did manual work in addition to prayer and meditation. Gandhi drew inspiration from a neighboring Trappist abbey that he had visited.

Gandhi left South Africa after a 1914 breakthrough in the battle for equal rights. He began his campaign to liberate India from British colonial rule. The Indians had fought with the British in WWI and were very disappointed not to be rewarded for their efforts with greater independence. Gandhi's South African victory gave him confidence that justice would prevail through nonviolent resistance. He founded an ashram in Ahmedabad and lived there for sixteen years. It became the center of the resistance. Members of the ashram took ten (later, fourteen) vows, including the vow of truth, nonviolence (*ahimsa*), celibacy, poverty, fearlessness, manual labor, religious tolerance, and the making of their own clothes. Communal prayer and work were practiced, a daily newspaper was published, and actions of nonviolent resistance were organized.

The two most famous such actions of Gandhi's movement were the fight against the British monopolies on cotton and, later, on salt. The great impact of these acts of civil disobedience was a result of their simplicity and universal accessibility. Everyone could understand and take part. The movement mobilized for the rights of women and 'untouchables,' the lowest caste in India's rigid social hierarchy. It also introduced the principles of a local, small-scale, and cooperative economy as an alternative to the colonial system of international trade. Gandhi wanted every family to have a spinning wheel, a small-scale technology that would enable Indians of all classes to make their own clothes and cease to be dependent on the British textiles made from Indian cotton.

With his famous salt march Gandhi fought a British monopoly that robbed Indians of control over their own resources. England's violently repressive response showed Indians that the colonizer perceived them as a threat, that is, a power to be reckoned with. When Gandhi spent some years in captivity, the movement of nonviolent resistance only grew. In 1942, Gandhi and the Congress Party launched the 'Quit India Movement.' This too was brutally repressed by the British. The Congress Party took the political lead in the pursuit of independence but, as Gandhi scornfully remarked:

"For the Congress Party, nonviolence was a tactic and not a spirituality." What worried Gandhi even more was the internal struggle between Muslims and Hindus, which would eventually lead to the 1947 partition of East and West Pakistan from India. Gandhi tried to prevent this separation, but was murdered by a nationalistic Hindu during a reconciliation meeting. More than a million Hindus and Muslims were killed during the subsequent battles.

Gandhi freed India from British colonial rule and stirred the self-consciousness of a nation. The fact that he did not achieve his dream of a nonviolent India does not make his principles any less relevant. We can map them onto our own time because we too must realise the transition from an oppressive economy to a sustainable life economy. Gandhi's unprecedented progress towards this same goal was based on three basic principles: *satyagraha, sarvodaya,* and *swadeshi.*

THE THREE BASIC PRINCIPLES

Satyagraha (derived from *satya,* truth, and *graha,* taking) stands for resistance to any form of falsehood and injustice. Gandhi believed that standing up for truth meant active resistance to insincerity and was linked to the ideal of nonviolence (*ahimsa*). Nonviolence was the spiritual power that freed the Indian people from colonial domination and motivated Gandhi to change the social and economic systems of South Africa and India. The *ahimsa* principle came to Gandhi from his mother, a Jainist, for whom nonviolence is a path towards spiritual purification and enlightenment. Gandhi's readings of Tolstoy and Henry Thoreau inflected the principle of nonviolence with an ecological and social meaning. *Ahimsa* expanded to a way of connecting with the earth and the oppressed in society. Schweitzer was sometimes critical of

Gandhi, but they shared the *ahimsa* ideal and its principle of respect for life.

In his autobiography, Gandhi characterizes his actions as *experiments with truth*. Truth reveals itself by doing and requires constant vigilant reflection and discernment. Therefore Gandhi regularly withdrew for a day of fasting and reflection. He regarded this not as a luxury but, rather, as a necessary basis for clear thinking and correct action. In addition to these regular days of withdrawal, he meditated every morning and evening. He moved around as much as he could on foot, allowing for conversation and reflection. He used his many days of imprisonment to read and to write down his ideas. His insights never claimed any absolute or exclusive truths. They were personal narrative accounts of how he came to understand and act.

Gandhi resisted absolute truth claims throughout his life. *His* truth, it could be said, was that no religion, science, or worldview had a monopoly on truth. Members of his ashrams had to take the vow of religious tolerance. The openness to truth as a dialogical process provided a spiritual basis for his political activities and economic reforms. He advocated a nonviolent economy of all for the good of all. Or, quoting E.F. Schumacher, "economics as if people mattered." (Schumacher, 1973) Gandhi's guiding principles for this nonviolent, participatory economy were: *sarvodaya* and *swadeshi*.

Sarvodaya (*sarva*, everyone; *udaya*, lift up) is usually translated as 'the welfare of all,' although 'progress for all' might be closer to the original sense. This principle was inspired by John Ruskin's book, *Unto this Last* (1862), which had been a guide for Gandhi in South Africa and which he translated into Gujurati. The principle can be broken down into three radical points:

- The good of an individual is included in the good of all;
- The work of a lawyer is worth as much as that of a barber and everyone has the same right to a decent wage;
- Voluntary manual labor is necessary to live a true life.

These three principles are the inverse of our modern economy, in which self-interest and 'my country first' are guiding forces; in which there is a growing income gap between 'white' and 'blue' collar professions; and in which manual labor is carried out by computers, robots, or otherwise avoided. Much of this was already true in Gandhi's time. The three principles were the signposts in the fight against the injustices of the colonial system. Not everything could be realized at once. Gandhi also made compromises, as in the case of the equal rights for the 'untouchables.' But his basic intuition always remained clear, as the following text inspired by Gandhi beautifully exemplifies (the text is borrowed from La Verna, Ghent):

Let us not call it progress,
To which another perishes.
Let us not call it growth,
From which another is diminished.
Let us not call it freedom,
Which deprives another of the right to be himself.
Let us not call it community,
Where the lesser does not get the greater attention.

Let us be the change
That we want to see in the world.

Swadeshi is self-reliance. In the struggle against the colonial rule this meant using local goods and a boycott of foreign products. Production by the masses instead of mass production. Today it would be called localization. The idea of a self-supporting economy is still very much alive in the *community-based organizations* that unite almost 100 million women in India (P. Santos 2017: 38). But I suspect that Gandhi would be very critical of our digital economy, empowering high-tech giants and big data systems while disabling human creativity. Digitalization in and of itself is not the problem. The problem is the dominance of monopolies and the reduction of consciousness to utilitarian thinking that follows in digitalization's wake.

Without a revaluation of small-scale and local production, without balancing efficiency with care, we will not realise the model of self-reliance (Jolien Noels: 2020). It is an illusion to think that we can just turn around the current logic of the domineering economy; great change requires a sustained effort by the many. Market and government regulation will not suffice to imagine and create an artisanal, local economy focused on the development of people rather than on the returns on capital and the quantitative growth of GDP. It could be argued that the 'social profit sector,' which promotes the principles of solidarity, subsidiarity, and the dignity of the person, incarnates the profile of the Gandhian economy. Unfortunately that sector to-day is itself too much beholden to market forces, to the urge for growth, financial returns, and the ability to meet market demands. An economy of hope must find new strategies to nurture small scale, craftsmanship, and sustainable economies of care and self-reliance. The Gandhian principles of non-violent resistance to untruth, progress for all, and self-reliance—and the great changes those lead to—can continue to inspire us moving forward.

CHAPTER 3

CARE AS HOPE

Care is a basic element of all life. Animals care for their offspring and for the survival of their species. Trees communicate with each other underground via fungi in the forest, hence taking care of the forest as a whole. Flowers and insects interact for mutual benefit. People also care for one another. Our planet as a whole is a complex network of mutually supporting balances; all life forms depend on each other in one way or another. Care is the transformation of that vulnerable codependency into a relationship of mutual support. Care increases the chances of survival for all involved, their zest for life, and resilience.

But we often see the other as the enemy and rely for survival on a desire for power and control over our environment. The 'flight and fight' response is deeply ingrained in our DNA. This does not mean that care is completely absent. Given the right circumstances, care and compassion can prevail over the instinct to dominate and control.

Humans usually understand care as a relationship of assistance: a care provider supports recipients who cannot support themselves. Systems of collective care simply expand this individual assistance model, allowing society to help its most vulnerable communities. But assistance can turn into paternalistic attitudes of power and control over the other. There is also the danger of reducing aid to the alleviation of material and social needs which, according to Maslow's Pyramid, must first be satisfied before 'higher needs' can be addressed.

What happens when institutions of care are instead organized from the perspective of hope? Hope both as an individual and social virtue has its origin in our desire for a meaningful future. But for its realisation it needs two wings. One is voluntaristic hope, which for all its many virtues, reduces care to problem solving. Its focus is to deliver services of care that alleviate well defined needs with the sole aim of getting people to the standards of 'normal' life. Such a frame of mind remains pragmatic and economic, with no place for the little girl, *espérance*. And yet she is essential. Meta-hope as the other wing is the ability to continue to trust that life has meaning despite all failure. Care then means paying attention to unsolvable problems, believing in the seemingly impossible, open-ended listening to the stories of people dreaming of another future. I am not proposing a conflict between two forms of hope. Efficiency and meaning, rationality and spirituality, must support one another. Meta-hope is the inspiring force that shifts boundaries and unlocks new goals from within. What would it mean to integrate the spiritual meta-hope in our (health) care?

WHAT DOES CARE MEAN?

Before addressing the interaction between hope and care it is useful to distinguish a few layers of meaning within the concept of care:

1. Care refers to a **service provided to a person in**

need, a definition encompassing a very wide range of activities—feeding a baby, caring for the sick, performing surgery, administering a vaccine, visiting a prisoner, welcoming migrants, and so on. The 'service' consists of a specific activity that supports the person in need due to illness, disability, or lack of power. This service can be translated into an algorithm, a program to be carried out by a robot. This will probably happen more and more often in the future.

2. Care in a developed society is not only provided by well-intentioned individuals. Care is also a **social system**, regulated by laws, controlled by authorities, and financed and accounted for in a legal way. At the level of financing and responsibility one can distinguish between profit-oriented and social-oriented regulation. The legal framework in the two cases is different, but this difference is becoming less relevant as the non-profit sector, a social entity, integrates more and more free market regulation and the profit-sector, a private entity, embraces more and more elements of moral and social regulation. Much more challenging today is the tension between care as a collective and bureaucratically organized system and care as an inter-personal and participative relationship.

3. Care is a **unique relationship** between a person in need and a caregiver. Although care as a specific service and a collective system can be described in a fairly technical and abstract way—care as a unique relationship cannot. Far more happens in a human relationship than the providing of a technical and reproducible service, or the application of legal rules and procedures. A human relationship, rather, is a living, reciprocal interaction between two people based on freedom, hope, and empathy. Care here means paying attention to *this* person, to the ever-shifting dynamics and context of *this* unique care request. And because the care relationship is

essentially asymmetrical—the person seeking care is dependent upon the means, information, and competence of the caregiver—it is also profoundly vulnerable. Because of this asymmetry there is always a real danger of an abuse of power, which can be partly countervailed by a framework of protective rules and partly by a culture of respect for the human person. Respect can be strengthened by the insight that the caregiver's power is fundamentally dependent on the person seeking care. Without people needing aid, after all, caregivers would have no status, income, or employment. Moreover every caregiver will sooner or later become themselves a person in need, confronted with suffering and death. This knowledge of shared vulnerability may create a culture of reciprocal respect. And this brings us to a fourth meaning of care.

4. Care is **a way of giving meaning to life and death**. I found a beautiful example of this meaning-giving power in Emily Esfahani Smith's book, *The Power of Meaning* (2017). She describes Dr William Breitbart doing research at the Cancer Institute in New York on how terminally ill people give, or do not give, meaning to their death and life. Some responded quite directly, saying essentially, 'If you want to help me, make sure I die.' However, Breitbart found that it was not pain that caused the demand for assisted suicide but the feeling that cancer had robbed life of its meaning. Inspired by psychiatrist Viktor Frankl's account of how a sense of purpose allowed him to survive the concentration camps (*Man's Search for Meaning*, 1946), Breitbart developed an eight-session care therapy:

> First session: ask to name one or two moments when they felt their life was meaningful. The second session consisted of questions about their identity before and after

the cancer diagnosis. In the third and fourth session they shared their life stories with the group. Session five was about the meaning of death: what would they consider a good death? Where would they like to die, how should their funeral be organized, and how do they want to be remembered. Session 6 and 7 are about the sources of meaning in their lives: what has given them meaning in life? To what extent have they reached their goal? Session 8 suggests formulating a 'legacy project' via a text, symbol, picture...

Research afterwards showed that the therapy worked. The therapy had clearly improved people's spiritual well-being. The demand for assisted suicide had virtually disappeared.

Another example of meaningful care is the practice of gratuity and thankfulness proposed by Joanna Macy and Chris Johnstone in their book, *Active Hope* (2016). Gratitude promotes cooperative behavior, as the following experiment demonstrates:

In the 1970s, Alice Isen set up an experiment by leaving coins in public phone boxes so that the next person who wanted to make a call would get a free call. When that person finished making the call and left the phone box, one of the researchers apparently accidentally dropped a stack of papers right in front of that person. This process was repeated at phone boxes where no coins had been placed. The people who received the unexpected gift of a free call were much more willing to help the researcher pick up her papers (Macy, 2016: 59).

CARE AS CREATION OF MEANING: A PHILOSOPHICAL DISPUTE

Care as hope places the spiritual factor, the fourth meaning of care, at the center. The order of the four care dimensions is in fact reversed—Maslow's Pyramid is turned on its head, the needs of the spirit no longer put off until those of the body have been satisfied. And this foregrounding of the intuitive sense of meaning invigorates our active capacity to explore new paths. The technical description of care as a product or system no longer defines but, rather, now comes *out of* our sense of purpose.

Let us stay here for a moment and dig deeper into meaningful care. I will confine myself to the differing views of two of the most important philosophers of the last century on this subject. Heidegger and Levinas have very different views on how care gives meaning. But what they have in common is the belief that the vulnerability of existence is the core of care (Bouckaert, 2019).

In his seminal text, *Sein und Zeit* (1927), the German philosopher Martin Heidegger claimed *Sorge* (care) as the fundamental structure of human existence. The ever-present foreknowledge of *my* death structures human life around a basic instinct of fear for its survival. Human effort may be able to postpone death and create a fragile space of freedom. We can try to shape (finite) time and write our (limited) history together, within the context of fear and threat that are, for Heidegger, essential. Life without them consists of erecting false securities that will inherently fail and wasting our time in idle talk. Those who flee from fear-for-death condemn themselves to just such an inauthentic life. Those who face their fear-of-death are thereby forced to use the short time allotted to them for a personal life project. For

Heidegger, care as a social service (*Fürsorge*) is only meaningful in the context of the existential care for our finite existence.

The Jewish-French philosopher Emmanuel Levinas was initially an admirer of Heidegger, but became one of his fiercest critics after the Holocaust. The core of his criticism is that the primary concern for one's own existence blinds us to the vulnerability of other people. This involvement with the suffering of others is, in turn, our only means for overcoming our fearful concern for our own life. Only when that suffering *touches me more deeply* than the concern for my own death will my egocentric fear-of-death give way to a liberating sense of solidarity and responsibility. My freedom is then not primarily determined by concern for myself. It is determined by concern for the concrete suffering of the particular other who crosses our path but who represents at the same time the suffering of every other.

Care for Levinas is an 'unchosen responsibility for the other.' We do not choose whom we help. The other is the vulnerable traveler who crosses our path. All attempts to avoid the meeting—like those of the priest and the Levite in the story of the Good Samaritan—inevitably fail. We are touched by the encounter and are faced with a choice. Either we, like the Samaritan, take care and transform our freedom into solidarity, or we scramble for excuses to avoid caring and flee in fright to the confines of our finite freedom. The exchange works both ways: the Samaritan gives the wounded traveler the necessary physical and financial support; the wounded traveler frees the Samaritan from his anxious and restless concern for his ego.

The differences between Heidegger's *Sorge* and Levinas' *responsabilité non choisie*, important as they are, should not overshadow the centrality of care to both thinkers. Both interpret care as a response to a touching experience of vulnerability. Heidegger focuses on the ontological fact that, as human beings, we are at the mercy of death. With Levinas the experience of vulnerability starts with being touched by someone else's suffering. For both, care is the effort to give sense and meaning to a traumatic experience. However, both philosophers over the years have corrected and complemented their views.

For Heidegger, the fear of death increasingly makes way for a different experience of our finitude, the experience that Being does not coincide with the actual world. Differently put: life is always *more* than all the actual forms of life. There is an indelible difference between the Being (Life) and the beings (forms of live) , which Heidegger calls the ontological difference. Being simultaneously unfolds itself as a source of meaning in 'beings' and retains its plentitude, which therefore remains hidden. That is to say that reality is not exhausted by its manifestations or by our efforts to understand it. There is always *more* to it than it can show or we can grasp, which is why life remains unpredictable, beyond (mere) comprehension. Hence also the consistent failure of modernity and science's attempts to reduce Being to a makeable and measurable world. For Heidegger, poets such as Hölderlin are 'caretakers' or guardians of the hidden Being, the sensors that detect the unexpected in events. Care in this context is also much broader than social assistance; it is first and foremost taking care for the hidden meaning in human and non-human beings.

Levinas is, once again, critical of this Heideggerian view of care. He thinks that Heidegger's view of Being as an unpredictable horizon that enlightens beings neglects the responsibility of human beings for each other. If Being is first of all an unpredictable horizon, one can go in any direction. It is therefore no coincidence for Levinas that Heidegger welcomed and supported the rise of Nazism and the Third Reich as a new and promising manifestation of Being. For Levinas meaning does not start with the experience of a horizon that makes everything possible but, rather, with the confrontation that '*not* everything is possible.' We are responsible for the suffering of the other and have a duty to bear and remedy it.

Is Levinas' critique of Heidegger advocating for an ethic of radical altruistic sacrifice? Do we not have a duty to take care of our own existence and to disclose new utopias of meaning and future (as Heidegger would say)? Levinas' answer is that self-care and caring for the future are 'second order' conditions. The first order is given by the face of the other. However, because there are so many faces that appeal upon our sense of compassion, we need to think in terms of equal rights and to balance our care. Without balance that also includes a sufficient form of self-care, we will do injustice to one or another person. The point is that in our rational thinking and organizing of rights and balance, we must never lose sight of our primary and direct experience of responsibility for the concrete other. We must remain alert for the immediate confrontations in which people address me in *personal* ways, not in anonymous manifestations of Being. Even a perfect care system that treats all people equally, will always to some extent neglect the other because every person and every context is unique. The 'little goodness' that, beyond the rules of the system, pays attention to the unique presence and suffering of a person is therefore an indispensable and foundational feature of authentic care for Levinas (Roger Burggraeve, 2020).

Heidegger's philosophy is often linked to an eco-metaphysics: Being as the creative power of nature sustains our world, while simultaneously making it unpredictable and beyond our control. Heidegger himself loved nature and wrote most of his philosophical works in his country house in the Black Forest. For him, a return to nature frees us from a destiny (*Seinsgeschick*) dominated by technology and science and makes us sensitive to the *Geheimnis*, the deeper meaning of Life.

What Levinas proposes is entirely different. No eco-metaphysics: not back to nature but back to the human face of the other.[1] Nature does not speak to us as a human face does. It is an anonymous and indifferent presence, not a measure of meaning. Nor does Levinas refer to future generations which is an abstract category. Of course we can project ourselves into a future situation, but this self-projection is not a confrontation with the immediate expression of a face. Levinas' strong focus on the human face as the basis for the experience of alterity and goodness leaves, I am afraid, little room for an authentic eco-spirituality.

So the question remains: how can we develop an eco-philosophy that (in contrast to Heidegger) takes the personal responsibility towards the other seriously and that (in contrast to Levinas) does justice to nature as a source for creation of meaning? I believe that in order to do this we must first deepen the idea of vulnerability which opens a possibility to experience our relationship to nature as an I-Thou relationship, to use the words of the famous Jewish philosopher, Martin Buber.

FROM SOCIAL TO ECOLOGICAL VULNERABILITY

Vulnerability is a marginal concept in modern Western philosophy because the latter is grounded on the ideal of human autonomy. Vulnerability is considered negatively because it reduces our autonomy and makes us dependent on others. Science, technology, and management are the modern tools to reduce this vulnerability and gain more control over ourselves and our environment. Although we can get some control over our dependencies, we never can eliminate them. We will always remain deeply dependent on nature for our food, light, energy, etc. Social interaction is dependent on trust in the other. And the condition we have the least control over, the greatest affront to our autonomy, is the fact that we all have to die. Vulnerability can be primarily defined as human dependence on unpredictable situations and agencies.

Modern economics reduces vulnerability to a scarcity problem. Greater productivity creates lesser dependence on the resources of other nations and, by generating the illusion of *infinite* resources, our environment. But our abundance creates new paradoxical sources of vulnerability, such as inequality, obesity, and stress. Something similar happens in politics. Politics sees vulnerability as an issue of power. By managing power democratically and redistributing it socially, individual freedom (autonomy) should grow while vulnerability lessens. Instead, new clusters of power concentration, exclusion, and inequality emerge—and with them new sources of vulnerability. It sometimes seems that vulnerability increases in inverse proportion to our efforts to eradicate it. Like the paradox of security: the more we pursue security, the more we feel threatened. Or another example: the more America and England attempted to create a stable world with their War on Terror, the more they achieved the exact opposite.

How can we change our negative perception of vulnerability? Let us return to Levinas and his awareness that the vulnerability of the other is not a physical or social restriction on my freedom, but an ethical one: I must not kill, even if I can. More than that, I must support the other; I have been given the unrequested responsibility of being their host. For Levinas this ethical 'hijacking' coincides with the 'epiphany of the human face.' How can we disconnect his ethic of responsible care from his 'philosophy of the face'?

In Dutch we have two words to express the French *visage*. *Aangezicht* (the face) expresses what we physically see: the eyes, ears, nose, mouth, etc. It is the physical instrument through which we communicate with each other in daily life. It creates conviviality and social life. Therefore the face should always remain visible in the public area. But *gelaat*, the other Dutch word for face/visage, refers to something invisible and more subtle. It refers to what we cannot express or communicate, something beyond control. It refers to the existential vulnerability of our being which we cannot overcome but which we can share with other persons. By allowing the face/*gelaat* of the other to touch my being and vice versa, it becomes *our* vulnerability. The face as *gelaat* opens a relational space for reciprocal responsibility, patience and care. It makes possible what is the essence of every authentic encounter: the sharing of each other's existential vulnerability.

Many people have experiences similar to that described by Levinas in their dealings with nature. Animals and trees, without the human face, can still touch us with their vulnerability. I found a quote from Emil Corian, the Romanian-French philosopher, which expresses it very well: "The individual exists only insofar as he amasses within himself the silent grief of things, of old rags as well as the cathedral. It is not I who suffer in the world, but the world that suffers in me." (Corian, source unknown) The suffering of animals and the vulnerable position of some endangered species, the earth disturbed by overexploitation, the stolen future of generations to come—all of this affects us as persons with the ethical imperative to engage. In the tearful face of the activist, Greta Thunberg, who calls on the United Nations to stop the abuse of the Earth, the vulnerability of the Earth indirectly takes on a human face. Nature, like the human being, has an alterity and vulnerability that 'hijacks' us and imposes an ethical responsibility even when we do not benefit from it. The human face is only one of the expressions of the vulnerability of Life.

MARTIN BUBER'S ECOLOGICAL INTERPRETATION OF THE I-THOU RELATIONSHIP

In 1923, the Jewish philosopher and mystic Martin Buber published his best-seller, *Ich und Du*. This book was a turning point. He had previously been strongly inspired by Schopen-hauer and Nietzsche, writing exuberant texts on the mystical experience (*Erlebnis*) of solidarity. The war and the criticism of his friend Landauer made him aware that mystical flow could easily degenerate into blind violence. He shifted his focus from the psychological *Erlebnis* to the interpersonal relationship.

> Erlebnis' belongs to the exclusive, individualized psychic sphere (...); 'Encounter' or better yet, 'relationship' radi-cally transcends this sphere. The psychological reduction of reality, its psychologisation, had a destructive effect on me in my youth because it removed me from the ground of human reality, the existence of 'one for another.' It was only much later, when the development of my thinking taught me to struggle and to look for a basis, that I discov-ered a reality that is never lost. (Buber in Mendes-Flor 1989:105; own translation)

The post-war Buber believed that in order to structure the world we use two 'root words' expressing two different types of relation. Whoever uses the root word I-Thou is involved in a inter-subjective relationship of reciprocal, and personal Presence (*Gegenward*). I-It, on the other hand, places an individual ego in relationship to an extrinsic object (*Gegenstand*), to the world as object-related experience. I-It relationships always involves the loss of the personal presence of the Other. What is 'gained' is distance, control, and the use of things. One would think that Buber, like Levinas, would at this point say that the world of things belongs to the I-It sphere and our social world to the I-Thou domain. This is how his work has often been superficially and wrongly interpreted.

Think of a tree. We can describe it precisely: its place and age, its nature and condition. We can compare it with other specimens. We can analyze and explain its functioning from biology. We can even determine its market value. In all this, the tree is an object, a *Gegenstand*. But Buber writes: "It can happen, both by will and by grace, that when I look at the tree I am drawn into a relationship with it, and then the tree is no longer an It. (...) The tree is no impression, no figment of my imagination, no value, but it faces me and relates to me, as I relate to it—only differently. (...) It is not the soul of a tree or a dryad that meets me, but the tree himself." (Buber, 2020: 12-13)

Buber's work mainly focused on the social context of the I-Thou encounter. His view on the relationship with nature and art is less well known. He returns to this topic in an afterword, thirty-five years later, by wondering how the reciprocity of the personal I-Thou encounter could take form in our relationship with plants, animals and things. Buber introduces a gradation here. With animals, and especially tamed animals, we can still quite easily develop a personal and interactive relationship. Moreover, there are people "who possess the capacity to be partners with animals—they are, by the way, not the 'animal people' but rather spiritually inclined." (Buber 2020:143). Just think of the many iconic stories of St Francis' dealings with wild animals. The reciprocity between animal and human is experienced differently by everyone but is real for those who place themselves in the I-Thou relationship with an animal. Reciprocity is less clear when we talk about plants and trees. And yet it exists: "the unity of the tree that withdraws from even the keenest gaze of those who only investigate, opens itself to the gaze of those who say You; when **that** human being is there allowing the tree as a whole to manifest its unity, the tree also manifests it." (Buber 2020: 144)

The relationship that Buber describes with the tree is not an ecstatic merger, an epiphanic loss of the self into nature. It is the transformation of an objectifying I-It into a personal I-Thou relationship. I suspect that the Japanese practice of 'forest bathing,' wherein one embraces and listens to a particular tree, must be something like this. "When the soul listens, everything speaks a living language." (G. Gezelle) Such moments in nature are usually brief, but they can profoundly determine our behavior and initiate a reciprocal process of healing. The fox says to the little prince: "If you make me tame, then we will need each other. Then you will be unique to me and I will be unique to you." (Antoine de Saint-Exupéry) Those who care for nature experience something of its self-healing power. It is not a "do ut des" relationship (I give in order to get) but a reciprocal gratuity and gift. About the Thou-Nature moments, Buber writes: "They cannot be forced. They are a grace, for which one must always be willing and which one can never acquire as a sure possession." (Buber 2020: 150)

In the thirteenth century, the dying Francis of Assisi composed his Song of the Sun, in which he considered the sun and the moon, water and fire, air and earth, suffering and death, to be his brothers and sisters. Partnership with nature in which God is actively present was part of Francis' way of thinking and living. The Buddhist Zen monk Thich Nhat Hanh puts it in his own words: "You carry Mother Earth inside you. She is not outside you. Mother Earth is not only your environment. In being intertwined (inter-being) it is possible to have real communication with the earth, which is the highest form of prayer."

Efficiency thinking driven by the I-It relationship cannot lead to a genuine partnership with nature. What Buber teaches us is that authentic care is always twofold. Professional competence requires, in addition to efficiency, attention to the personal presence of each living being. Reciprocity is essential, although it can take very different and subtle forms. Buber points out that in therapeutic or educational settings there can never be complete reciprocity. 'Normatively limited reciprocity'—emphatic attention, but at a distance—make healing and education possible. It allows us to combine compassion with professional competence. In the next section we will discuss the story of Dr Rediger and his research into the explanation of sudden healings. It illustrates Buber's view of the dual nature of our relationship to nature, as both an object of research and a healing partner.

MEDICINE OF HOPE (J.REDIGER)

Today many voices advocate an integral or holistic health care system. Interdisciplinary teams pay attention to the interaction of social, psychological, and biochemical aspects in diseases. But there are still many blind spots and many questions. How holistic is organized healthcare today? How much attention do we pay to the ecological context in which we live? Is illness just about pain and inflammation or are these just symptoms of a deeper failure of our immune system?

A health system only changes fundamentally when the idea of illness and health changes. This is well illustrated by the famous case study of the Hungarian-Austrian surgeon, Ignaz Semmelweiss. At the beginning of the nineteenth century, Semmelweiss sought an explanation for the fact that an average of 25% of women died of maternal fever after giving birth. His attention was particularly triggered by the fact that in his own clinic the figure was noticeably higher in one ward than in another. How to explain this significant difference? The prevailing conclusion at the time was that diseases 'spontaneously arise' in the female organs. Semmelweiss' investigations led him to an alternative hypothesis, that the cause of the higher mortality rate in one of the wards was the fact that medical students came to work in the infamous ward with unwashed hands after a lesson in anatomy. He forced them to wash their hands with a mixture of chlorine and lime, resulting in a sharp drop in the mortality rate. Semmelweiss believed that disease did not arise spontaneously in the organs, but was transmitted by micro-organisms that remained stuck to the hands. He enforced a strict hand washing discipline.

But if disease was caused by a bacterium, rather than arising spontaneously, then doctors themselves became the cause of death. The idea was hence met with so much resistance that Semmelweiss finally had to resign. He was declared insane and admitted to the psychiatric institution in which he would die. Many years—and many more unnecessary deaths—had to pass before 1862, when Pasteur could experimentally prove that germs are microscopic creatures that can infect us through the air. The theory of the 'spontaneous onset' of disease was abandoned, leading to a change in medicine and hygienic practices. Antibiotics have long since been the drug of choice to kill pathogens. The view that disease is caused by infection is now globally accepted.

In a remarkable book, *Spontaneously Healing. In search of the source of our self-healing capacity* (2021), Doctor Jeffrey Rediger (psychiatrist and lecturer at Harvard Medical School) explores the capacity of people to heal in a 'miraculous way' by changing their self-image and identity. Because conventional medicine ignores the extraordinary phenomenon of spontaneous remissions, preferring to focus on statistical averages, Doctor Rediger decided to critically investigate the matter himself. Since 2003 he has systematically collected and investigated stories of spontaneous healing and interviewed those involved. He has documented case studies of medically hopeless cancers and chronic diseases that were suddenly cured. What Rediger discovers is that all these spontaneous healings do not just happen 'spontaneously.' They show a certain pattern. The response of these people to their hopeless and out-of-touch situation is to make radical changes in their lives. They try to 'reset' their lives and their relationships in function of the time they have left. This mental and emotional reaction *in some cases* awakens the immune system, enabling it to quickly and effectively eliminate the life-threatening bacteria and viruses.

Doctor Rediger's research further shows that this 'transformation' is linked to a whole series of concrete actions, such as different eating habits, eliminating stress, letting go of destructive relationships, offering forgiveness, taking up meditation and prayer, and accepting death. All of these are activities and behaviors that express the person's new relationship with both their environment and with themselves. None of these changes by themselves appear to be adequate for any 'miracle cure.' But the combination of them all and the will of the person concerned to choose a new path seems to be capable of just that.

> What these cases teach us is that we need to create a biological environment in the mind and body that paves the way for healing. The body ultimately wants to heal. It takes more to create the conditions for that than we have been taught (...) Where (the research) finally took me was to the foundation of a new model of medicine, one that is based on what I now call the 'four pillars' of health: healing your immune system, healing your nutrition, healing your stress reaction and healing your identity (Rediger 2021: 25).

According to Doctor Rediger, the most important and decisive factor in such unexpected and radical healing processes is the fourth: the ability to heal your identity or personality. This healing capacity also has a neurobiological basis. We could call it the 'black box' in our brains. Or, more scientifically, the default mode network (DMN), a collection of brain areas that are loosely connected and light up when you are occupied with thoughts that have to do with your conscious or unconscious self-perception. This 'I'-network is built out of the experiences and traumas of our past, which have become ingrained in our brains. If this network is very negative, harmful, or restrictive it can completely disorient our biological system. This neurological ego-system is usually considered to be fixed or permanent. But the examples of 'spontaneous healers' show that this system can be changed. The great thing about the term *default mode network* is that it accurately captures "how identity is partly a function of nerve endings and pathways that can be altered or redrawn, just as a map can be altered or redrawn as a landscape changes over time." (Rediger 2021: 300)

In the final chapter of his book, Rediger outlines how the doctor of the future can become a real health coach using the possibilities offered by Artificial Intelligence. "The doctor's task is to connect, understand, see the full picture of the patient, and compassionately tailor care to their specific experience of the world." (Rediger 2021: 392) Doctor Rediger ends his book with a plea for a medicine of hope.

> We need hope in medicine. Fortunately, it is already there. Hope is there in the stories of people who have overcome incurable diseases. It is there in the doctors, nurses and surgeons who actually practice a medicine of hope; how difficult it is for them to work in and against a system that is geared towards increasing disease, towards treating with magic bullets, rather than increasing health from the ground up. Hope is there in the scientific studies, hidden away by the averages, but it is still there. Look for the exceptions. Look for the points on the outside of the graph. Don't let them be buried by the law of averages. They are there, and more than we think. Believe that you can be one of those exceptions if that is what you really want. Make sure your careers help you to make that happen. (Rediger 2021: 395)

There is a clear and major limitation in Doctor Rediger's research. His research selects successful case studies of sudden healing. We learn almost nothing about possible cases of people who made similar efforts but did not heal. Either they do not exist, which would strongly support Doctor Rediger's plea for holistic medicine; or they do exist, which would prove that the explanation is somewhat more complex than what Doctor Rediger proposes. But despite this limitation, his work remains an inspiring reference point. Our care for each other can only gain from it.

CONCLUSION

What our reflection on care as hope brings us is fourfold:

One. Care is much more than the provision of assistance organized by subsidized services and products for people in need.

Two. Care as Hope places emphasis on the meaning-giving function of care. After all, hope is the ability to give meaning to death and life and to orient our care relationships on that basis. With Levinas, we discovered that this hope and meaning creation only works fully when we allow ourselves to be touched by the vulnerable face of the other (which includes *all* others). Fearful, calculating, self-care fixates us onto the impossible utopia of securing our own lives, which paradoxically increases rather than decreases the feeling of insecurity.

Three. Levinas' exclusive focus on the human face marginalizes the fragility of nature. Martin Buber gives us a key to restore our lost relationship with nature. By thinking and especially experiencing nature in the fundamental pattern of the I-Thou relationship, nature meets us as a meaningful 'partner' instead of as an object of use.

Four. Dr Rediger's analysis of spontaneous remissions in medicine shows us how a spiritual connection with nature and ourselves can deeply affect our self-perception and our immune system and explain in some cases what we call "miracles."

CHAPTER 4

ECONOMY OF HOPE

Is an 'Economy of Hope' just an illusion? The Greeks thought it could be far worse, the ultimate evil unleashed by opening Pandora's box. The reasoning behind this dire prophecy was that hope creates expectations that often turn out to be misleading. The 'yes-we-can' feeling may be initially inspiring but, after becoming tangled in contradictions and encountering obstacles, can lead the optimist far from their intended destination. A serious 'Economy of Hope' project is therefore not possible without first addressing the limits of hope. Kant urged exactly this project, a critical questioning of the possibilities of hope-filled thinking.

KANT'S THIRD QUESTION

According to Kant, three major questions confront a philosopher: What can I know? What must I do? What can I hope for? Kant's strategy was to examine first how our human faculties are functioning before addressing the 'what question.' To answer the question 'what can I know,' for instance, Kant carefully examines how the human faculty of knowledge is able to function and what are its limits. He did something similar for our moral judgement. The ethical question 'What must I do?' requires understanding of the human faculty of moral discernment. Kant's research gave us two of the most famous books in Western philosophy: *Critique of Pure Reason* (1781) and *Critique of Practical Reason* (1788).

Kant was less successful with his investigation of the third question; he never wrote a *Critique of Hope*. A rough outline of what that work might have looked like, however, is given in his third and lesser known, *Critique of Judgment* (1790). In it, Kant explains how we humans have, besides our theoretical and moral reason, a separate faculty of aesthetic and teleological judgment. In contrast to moral and scientific statements, these judgments are expressions of subjective taste (Kant's initial title for his work was, *Critique of Taste*), but Kant believed that our judgments of taste were not arbitrary. They are based on reflection, there is logic in them.

The judgment that something is beautiful, sublime, or meaningful is made with the belief that other people *ought* to agree with this judgment—even though it is known that many will not. We are not satisfied with the self-evidence of our emotions and subjective states. We try to get others to agree with us that this painting or this sunset is beautiful and *necessarily so*. The Mona Lisa is not beautiful because of its worth or number of visitors but, rather, because of some ineffable and yet intrinsic quality. This judgment is not based on scientific or moral reasons but refers implicitly to a *sensus communis*—a community of taste.

This is also true when we believe that nature is a source for the creation of meaning. While science analyses things causally and rationally, we, as spiritual beings, also search for a deeper purpose (*telos*) and destination in reality. In this capacity, we search for what we call the 'intrinsic meaning' of things, which can only be perceived with the subjective eyes of our mind. In short: both in art and eco-philosophy we start a priori from the idea that the world is more than a mechanically determined construction. By the power of our judgment we prove to ourselves that we live within a space wherein we can disclose purpose in life and nature. *Culture* is the expression of this striving for a meaningful and open world where our human freedom finds its destiny.

That one of the pillars of the Enlightenment, a champion of rational thought, should show us the connection between hope, meaning, and art might seem remarkable. But the image of Kant as constricted by an obsession with reason can't survive a reading of his *Critique of Judgment*. He is very clear in stating that the human mind cannot be reduced to algorithms or a set of ethical rules. The mind has more capabilities than that. With its spiritual insight and imagination, it is able to discover meaning and purpose in life. Hope is based on the conviction that we are part of a meaningful whole that transcends us.

It is worthwhile to reread some other Western Enlightenment philosophers from this perspective. Adam Smith, the father of economic thinking, places the origin of moral judgment in our mental capacity for empathy (*Theory of Moral Sentiments*, 1759). This is different from Kant's thinking, wherein the pure moral judgment rests on the legislative power of universal principles and not on our subjective sense. For Kant, aesthetics is the realm of the subjective—for Smith, all forms of thinking originate in their respective feeling (including science and morality!).

But behavior guided by subjective feelings of hope, as it all too often is, can also lead to anarchy and violence. *De gustibus non est disputandum.* We will never agree on tastes. How then can a link be established between taste and truth? Kant formulated this question as to the extent to which spiritual judgments of taste can guide us. Hannah Arendt, best known for her criticism of totalitarian thought, endeavors to answer it. Arendt was raised in Königsberg, the city Kant lived his entire life, and seeks from him a foundation for her critical thinking. Like Kant, she believes that science and morality are an insufficient foundation for hopeful thinking. Facts and principles are important, but a philosophy of life cannot exist without an inner, subjective truth.

Hannah Arendt believed that the 'spiritual organ of taste' acts in realms other than those of art and natural philosophy. She differed with Kant, and agreed with Adam Smith, in making it the core of socio-political life (Arendt, 1992). Through empathy and dialogue, we can make our personal and intuitive judgments more representative and thus more global (in the sense of inter-subjective). Open public debate is thus the pre-eminent place where we test our opinions. We learn to look at reality from many points of view, making our subjective convictions more internally consistent and externally representative. Hope-oriented thinking, therefore, always presupposes a form of discernment created by a collective, not an individual. Just as science requires an ongoing process of *evidence-based* research to prove or disprove theories, so do 'thinkers of hope' appeal to an *inter-subjective, experience-based* process of discernment to distinguish true from false hope.

When we talk about an economy of hope, it is important to distinguish the nature of the thinking on which our hopes are based. Neither scientific analysis nor even morality are the ultimate references. The source is to be found in what Kant called 'judgment,' and what we today like to call 'spiritual discernment.' Spirituality refers to the capacity of human beings to disclose a universal and hope-oriented meaning in their lives. Without activating this spiritual capacity, without thinking outside materialistic constraints, I fear that an Economy of Hope will never transcend efficiency thinking masquerading as hope.

The source of hope may lie in our faculty of judgment and spiritual discernment but *what* that hope entails remains unaddressed. What do we hope for, what is its main outlook and goal to realise? In general terms, hope is the virtue that points us to the future. Hope means being alert to what has not yet been born (Erich Fromm, 1968). An Economy of Hope therefore requires spiritual thinking that is directed towards the creation of a future. But what kind of future?

THINKING FROM THE FUTURE

With the reference to a future as the goal of hope, we come closer to the field of economics. Decisions in the realm of business, investment, the stock market, and so on, are determined by short- and long-term expectations. The rational *homo economicus* in each of us strives to optimize their happiness in a planned way. It is precisely for this reason that we tend to reduce the ever-elusive future to a controllable, measurable, and manageable concept. This of course fails. The future, far from being 'solved,' presents itself as one unexpected problem after another—and we live from one frustration or crisis to another, a constant string of disappointments of which economy is the 'science.' If we want to escape from living according to this sad science, as economics is sometimes called, an Economy of Hope must define 'future' differently than in terms of rational maximization.

Broadly speaking, we can distinguish three ways of thinking about the future: prognosis, utopia, and hope.

1) **Prognosis** is what we are most familiar with: the scientific forecast. International panels of climate scientists

measure the rise of CO_2 on our planet based on actual data and predict the related consequences. Their understanding of the causes also shows us how to limit our carbon emissions. With Covid-19, statisticians and virologists predicted what to expect and told us how to combat it. Of course, it is only when the future we have hoped for is threatened that we turn to science. Scientific research into the future of insects, for example, will be of little interest to us unless we really care about biodiversity (or when a plague of locusts, or Asian hornets, threatens). The future we desire determines what science and research we deem relevant. Our desired future also impacts the selection of concepts and data by the researchers.

2) Whereas scientists see the future as a measurable projection based on current data and methods of analyses, utopian thinkers look for the ideal future. A **utopia** is not a forecast, nor an extrapolation of facts. It is a product of our imagination, a visionary projection of our deepest wishes. The urtext of utopian thought is Thomas More's *Utopia*, published over five hundred years ago in Leuven (1516). But utopia as a philosophical and literary concept has existed much longer. Plato, without knowing the word, designed a model of an ideal society (*The State*, 318 BC). He soon found out that his model was at odds with reality. He was twice invited by the tyrant of Syracuse to apply his ideal blueprint there, but resistance proved much greater than the willingness to live in such an enlightened state. In later dialogues, Plato made a number of proposals to narrow the gap between the actual and the desired society. But it was of little avail.

The gap between utopias and the world most of us live in usually leads to their dismissal as fantasies. But that does not prevent them from having a great social impact. Revolutionary spirits use utopias to change the course of history, for better or worse. As a result, although they originate as inspiring ideas, they often end up as nightmares. The young Marx and Engels of *The Communist Manifesto* argued for a classless society inevitably arising from a proletarian revolution, but Lenin, Stalin, and Mao translated this ideal into a state dictatorship controlled by the Communist Party. The consequences for those who did not fit the revolutionary blueprint were, and are, horrific.

Ideally, prognosis and utopia should balance each other out. There must be a systematic confrontation of the dream of an ideal society with the facts. Out of this process would emerge a plan for the transition from the actual to the desired society. A vision of utopia, with its problems forecasted and planned for, seems an ideal method for an economy of hope. But the future is unpredictable, refusing to be caught in the web of our forecasts, utopias, and transition plans. The future is more than a projection of facts. The term 'fact' is even misleading here, because as long as something does not exist, it is by definition not a fact. The future is a non-fact. Nor does the future coincide with our ideals, as history rarely follows the path of our ideals. How then can we think *from* the future? Hope is a third way.

3) In my book, *Choose Hope. How spirituality can transform the economy* (2017), I tried to show how **hope** comes from a deeper level than facts and ideals. Hope connects us to the creative dynamic of time. Hannah Arendt called this capacity of time to innovate, *the natality of time.* In opposition to much of classical philosophy, which focuses on the finiteness of time, this conception focuses our attention on time's capacity to *create something new.* Time as a source of unpredictable creativity, as an open horizon. Our intuitive and reflexive awareness allows us to connect spiritually to this

time dynamic, even though we do not know where it will lead us.

Time as an open horizon differs from mechanical, historical, or biological clock time. These forms of time display a more or less fixed and repeatable course. They make time measurable, predictable, and manufacturable, a certain degree of which is absolutely necessary for living together. The experience of time in hope, however, transcends these constrictive time frames. In twentieth century philosophy this 'time in hope' was central to such fundamental works as Henri Bergson's, *l'Evolution Créatrice* (1907); Heidegger's, *Sein und Zeit* (1927); and Alfred North Whitehead's, *Process and Reality* (1929). In the realm of business ethics, the concept is found in the German-American professor Otto C. Scharmer's, *Theory U. Leading from the future that presents itself* (2008). In his book, Scharmer clarifies how we can integrate the future as a source of meaning in processes of leadership and management, which we will examine in the next chapter.

But I would like to first emphasize one more point. The essentially unknown quality of the future must have a place in how we think about the future. We must strive to connect with this 'unknown' instead of reducing the future to a projection of what we already know or what we wish for. *Dare not to know*[1] is an argument for humility in our thought and honesty about the complexity and intractability of wicked problems.

But there is a caveat here. Openness for the future can have different roots, as we have seen in the dispute between Heidegger and Levinas in chapter 3. Our openness can be rooted in the belief that Being always transcends all particular forms of being. Because of this *ontological* difference (Heidegger), everything is possible and the ultimate future is beyond managerial control. The other way of interpreting openness is to look at it as an ethical responsibility to change history for and with all other living beings. The unknown here is the vulnerable presence of the other transcending all my ideas, ambitions, and self-projections, and requiring my future commitment. Because of this *ethical* difference that expresses the priority of the other over myself, not everything is possible. I am responsible for the good of the other, even if I don't fully know what the consequences are or how to take up this burden. Time is the space I get to change history for and with the other.

PRACTICES OF AN ECONOMY OF HOPE

The following two examples will help us understand the dynamics of hope: the older but still very relevant story of Ricardo Semler and the more recent Drawdown project by Paul Hawken.

Ricardo Semler is a Brazilian entrepreneur who took over the family business, Semco, in the 1980s. The industrial company was under heavy pressure. Ricardo's father had run the business according to the classic model of top-down management and strict hierarchy. Between 1980-1991, Ricardo instead sought to abolish all hierarchical structures. He allowed his employees to set their own working hours, organize their own work, and negotiate their own salaries. He familiarized everyone with the basic principles of book-keeping and balance-sheet reading, provided insight and over-sight into all results, and communicated all business plans and problems with the utmost transparency. A cynic might say Ricardo had run out of steam, thrown up his hands, turned the business over to others, and walked away. But the exact opposite is true.

In one of his books (because Semler now had time to write

books), *The Seven-Day Weekend* (2003), Semler discusses the principle of *leading by omission*. This echoes the Taoist *wu-wei*, the art of not-doing and not-knowing. Semler's version consisted of delegating as much as possible to his employees. He advocated for strong forms of economic democracy, creating a space in which workers' imaginations and creative capacities were challenged and optimized: "In a factory where everyone is financially involved in its success, the idea of asking subordinates to choose their future bosses themselves makes perfect sense." Keep in mind that this was not a small ICT company, but an industrial company with several thousand employees (approximately 5000 in 2010). That this democratic self-management worked and continues to work demands our serious attention.

Semler was convinced that the key to the future lay in a different way of working and connecting with people. Those who find pleasure in work enjoy the week as a seven-day weekend. Of course, there have to be results. But these are more a consequence than a goal. Job satisfaction is mainly the result of autonomy, trust, having time to experiment, work-life balance, and so on—productivity is only an auxiliary benefit. Semler's first objective was to give work meaning. He did so by creating an environment in which that meaning could be generated. The unexpected successes, encounters, and setbacks of those who worked in this environment could then inspire others to traverse the same terrain, and also find meaning therein. Within *this* working space chance, 'serendipity' (the ability to discover valuable things by chance), and intuition are allowed to enhance the quality of the experience, the product, and the profits—for all involved.

He writes that intuition "easily leads to mistakes, but probably less often than mathematical decisions." (Semler 2003:250) Traditional businesses use information to make forecasts; Semler uses information as a tool to support intuition. We do not need to waste our time with meticulously worked out long-term plans. Not only do they not work out, they also prevent us from thinking flexibly. It is far more important to stay permanently in touch with the living future. This is what Otto C. Scharmer calls *presencing* and what Ricardo Semler calls "rambling into the future or visiting the future." (Semler 2003:233) Wandering into the future without setting an a-priori goal is not, however, a blind wandering. It is 'thinking without handles' (H.Arendt), connecting with and allowing one's course to be influeced by the hope and moral intuitions of people.

A more contemporary example is Paul Hawken's Drawdown project. What makes this project so unique and hopeful is the fact that it successfully combines the three ways of thinking about the future: prognosis, utopia, and hope. The subtitle of Hawken's bestseller—*Drawdown. The Most Comprehensive Plan Ever Proposed to Reverse Global Warming* (2017)—is to some extent misleading, as the author himself points out in his introducing commentary:

> Our organization has not made or outlined a plan. This is beyond our capacity and we have not given ourselves such a mandate. In our research, we found a plan, a blueprint already present in this world in the form of collective human wisdom. This manifests itself in a variety of useful practices and technologies that are accessible to all, economically viable and scientifically validated (Hawken, 2017. X).

The so-called 'plan' differs from other climate plans in at least two important ways. First, it does not start from the fear of a catastrophe. Global warming is not a fatal disaster: *global warming is happening for us.* It is an atmospheric transformation that inspires us to change and rethink everything we do and make. It requires permanent discernment with the use of science and experiential knowledge. The study itself selects 100 projects and ranks them in order of efficiency to reach the drawdown point, that is, the point where global warming has peaked and is turning into a downward trend. But alongside the collection of scientifically validated projects, room is also left for the not-knowing, for the unexpected. In the last part of the book, under the title, *Coming Attractions*, projects (20% of all those cited in the book) are presented which are not yet fully science-based but supported by speculative knowledge.

The second distinguishing feature is the democratic character of the entire project. Paul Hawken attaches great importance to language and communication: the project is not aimed at specialized scientists but at the general public. The staff consists of scientists and writers. Also involved are a network of young research fellows, often advanced and competent students in various fields; a group of 'essayists' with a feel for the broader dynamics of society; and finally, a Board of Directors and a group of supporting foundations. The project works with a relatively limited budget.

Drawdown impressed me with a credible and hard-earned hope. The first page of the book features an iconic photo of a young girl from northern Kenya. Here the unknown future does not have a scientific plan but, rather, a human face. "Her picture has been our talisman calling us daily to the work that we do." (Hawken, 2017:XI) Here we see and encounter Charles Péguy's 'little girl hope.'

When the SPES forum launched the Economics of Hope project two years ago, it was based on the conviction that in times of crisis, the spiritual methodology of not-knowing—or, to put it more positively, the dynamics of hope—must find a place in scientific research, economics, and politics. Instead of allowing ourselves to be paralyzed by fear of the unknown, it is better—as in the Drawdown project and in the Semler story —to take the unknown as an inspiring starting point for transforming history for and with people.

CHAPTER 5

SPIRITUALITY AS 3D ETHICS

Most entrepreneurs would scoff at the words 'business spirituality.' They are more likely to talk about values and purpose or about corporate social responsibility. These concepts can be incorporated in policy instruments such as a value charter, a mission statement, or a CSR policy. Is corporate spirituality therefore a superfluous, perhaps even self-contradictory, concept? One of the first efforts to tackle that question in the European context was an international seminar in July 2001 organised by Business Ethics Center of Budapest. As an outcome of this productive workshop and the publication 'Spirituality and Ethics in Management' (2000), the European SPES Forum was founded.

Corporate spirituality leads us beyond 'values and norms' or 'goals and plans.' Jochanan Eynikel calls it, "the invisible undercurrent." (Check In, 2020) This undercurrent moves and inspires the visible course of the company. Or we may compare spirituality with 3D technology—what the latter does to our experience of space, spirituality does to our experience of time. It creates a depth dimension in our temporal perspective. Not only the short and long term get attention, but also the unknown from which the future emerges.

If we want to clarify the nature of spiritual theory and practice in business, it is important to anchor them in the basic experience of entrepreneurship. But as important as it is, the social context in which business takes place is also no vacuum. Deep inner changes are always connected with outer changes in society. When we founded the SPES-forum in 2000 as a local and international network for more 'Spirituality in Economy and Society,' we lived in a context of business scandals and the failure of neoliberal globalization. Therefore let us first explore the context in which corporate spirituality emerged before clarifying its core meaning.

CONTEXT

Two turning points deserve our attention. The first happened in the 70s and 80s of the last century, when the neoliberal deregulation of markets led to globalization. The second tipping point occurred at the beginning of this century and is now showing the limits of globalization.

'Business ethics' emerged as a movement for more Corporate Social Responsibility (CSR), a reaction to the rapidly increasing globalization of the 1970s and 1980s. The power of multinational companies increased at the expense of national governments losing their redistributive grip on the economy. The much-praised 'Rhineland model' was stalling. This model is based on close cooperation between government, social dialogue, and the free market, whereby the market provides competition and growth while the government and social dialogue take care of a fair redistribution. Progressive taxes and social security systems must reduce inequality while simultaneously ensuring the amount of purchasing power necessary for consumer demand to support economic growth.

So far, so good. But with the loss of power of the nation states through globalization, a vacuum is created. Who will ensure fair redistribution? How will they enforce it? A new form of social correction is needed to maintain confidence in the global machinery. NGOs, with the help of the media, mobilized behind ethical investment, calling on consumers to boycott unethical products and companies. Progressive entrepreneurs anticipated the changes and, whether altruistically or profit motivated, sought forms of ethical self-regulation. They advocated a model of corporate social responsibility (CSR) that, while corrective at the micro level, failed to prevent the major corporate scandals of the early 2000s (culminating in the bankruptcy of the US energy company, Enron, and, closer to home, the collapse of the speech technology company, Lernout&Hauspie). In 2008 the opaque and risky investment products offered by the banks led to another crisis and hence a new tipping point. Business ethics as 'moral self-regulation' had proved unable to reconcile the economy with the common good.

Today we have quite abruptly been confronted with several, mutually-reinforcing crises. Less acute but far more dangerous than the financial crisis are the consequences of the economy's long-term ecological over-exploitation. Climate change dominates the media. Greta Thunberg gave the protest a bitter face: the young generation rightly feels its future is mortally threatened. Social boundaries have simultaneously been breached. In *The Triumph of Injustice* (2020), Zucman and Saez, two economists who study the unequal distribution of income and wealth in the tradition of Thomas Piketty, come to the conclusion that in 2018, the 400 richest people in the US for the first time ever paid less tax on their income (23%) than the 50 percent lowest earners (24% on average). This is a massive shift from fifty years ago, when the richest were handing a far higher percentage of their income over to the government. This increasing inequality fuels the interminable and very well justified frustration and protest of the middle and lower classes in several western countries. The surplus value realized through globalization vanishes into the pockets of the rich. Not that everyone who wears a yellow jacket has read Marx, nor need they—the injustice and inequality is plain for all to see. The coronavirus entered into this already catastrophic situation, spreading rapidly through the network of global transactions and paralyzing the already fragile global economy. The war in Ukraine has decimated supply chains and long-held balances of power. How will humanity respond?

One possibility is a return to a version of the 'Rhineland model' with a strong government, more national borders, more local economy, more protection, and more self-defense. But closing borders has always led to more problems than it has solved. Closing borders closes minds, halts the import of new ideas and ways of living, strengthens defensive self-interest, and creates a polarized, hostile world. If the horrors of the last century have not taught us how explosive such a situation is, what will? And is there an alternative? Is it possible to create an 'open' Rhineland model? Who can/should develop that alternative?

We expect a lot from politics. But there are unfortunately not enough institutions that have the authority and power to balance the tension between globalization, justice, and ecology. Into this political vacuum step populist leaders seeking a return to national protectionism and self-interest. They promise that people will be masters in 'their homes' again. The reaction is understandable but worrying because in a digital world where everyone is connected and every economic project has global consequences, everyone's home is a shared space in which no one is the sole master.

What does spirituality and especially business spirituality mean in this context? Our not having a ready answer to this question is in itself a clue to the answer: historically, spiritual movements usually develop when there is a prevailing feeling in a society that the problems have become 'unsolvable,' that we desire things we cannot realize, and that we are stuck. Social and economic change occurs in the same charged environment.

CAN SPIRITUALITY SAVE THE WORLD?

Spirituality does not offer plans or blueprints that will solve the crisis or save the world—we (spiritual) humans have to do so. What spirituality does is provide a *method of thinking that is aimed at opening up a new future*. More about that method later. First, it should be clear that entrepreneurship and spirituality meet at this very point: they are both aimed at creating 'something new.'

In 1997, *Disclosing New Worlds* was published by three authors, a linguist (Spinosa), an entrepreneur (Flores), and a philosopher (Dreyfus). Inspired by the existential philosophy of Heidegger they started from the conviction that entrepreneurship is first and foremost a process of giving meaning, the 'art of making history.' The authors extend their discussion of entrepreneurship in business to political, social, and cultural organizations. True entrepreneurs are people with a strong contextual overview. They sense what is missing and are fascinated by new, unexplored possibilities. For example, Gillet, the inventor of the razor blade, was convinced that his invention was in line with a new cultural sense of efficiency and would replace the existing cumbersome ritual of shaving and its associated sense of masculinity. Entrepreneurship as 'the art of developing new ways of living' is very different from the rational management view that sees entrepreneurship as the 'ability to make a profit in competitive markets.' The focus is different. Instead of considering efficiency, competition, marketing, and management as the goal of business, the genuine conception of entrepreneurship requires attention to contextual dynamics, to what is not there yet, to the creation of new markets, to imagination, self-criticism, and dialogue.

A true entrepreneur sees a different world than a strict adherent to the 'fundamental tenants of business.' The first automobiles, for example, were not the result of successful, cost-efficient management in competitive markets. There were no markets for cars at that time and there was no demand for such unknown and non-existent vehicles. The first automobile created both a new product and a new demand that changed our mobility, our lifestyle, and our environment. The same applies to the first telephones, the first computers, the first credit cards, etc. None of these innovations came in response to a given market demand, nor have they been the result of cost-efficiency or marketing activities. They have been the result of innovative entrepreneurs with imagination and a sharp sense of people's aspirations.

Of course, rational management is necessary in any organization. No company can succeed without a clear definition of goals, a cost-effective use of resources, and an alertness to market opportunities. But these elements do not touch the moment of meaning-creation by which something that is not yet given emerges. Creating something new is 'moving a stone in the river': designing a product or service that makes life better and opens a new market. Precisely because of this creativity, entrepreneurship is more art than science, albeit an art that takes place in the space of free and competitive markets. Those who prioritize management will tend to restrict creativity as much as possible to streamlined objectives and rational processes; those who prioritize meaning creation will leave more room for the unexpected—the latter is of course the fertile ground for innovation.

How can we unlock spirituality as a source of entrepreneurial creativity? A first indispensable condition is the discovery of the spirit as a unique, human faculty. Unfortunately our capacity for spiritual thinking is all too often supplanted by our reliance on an economic rationality that strives for logical knowledge to guide our behavior according to the principle of enlightened self-interest, aiming at its best for the maximum long-term benefit for all. Anything that goes against this reason (*ratio*) is irrational. What is forgotten is that there are other meta-rational sources of knowledge that can guide us in times where everything is uncertain, ambiguous, and changing; conditions and context that make it impossible even to predict and to calculate long term benefit. Unlike our analytical and calculating mind (*ratio*), the spirit unlocks reality *as a whole* and by intuition opens a perspective in reality. The spirit can be experienced as a point in our consciousness that connects us in an intuitive way with everything, or more precisely with the soul of everything. In touch with it, we feel the flow of Life as it develops in an infinity of different forms, none of which it ever completely coincides with, and even this great abundance never exhausting its plenitude. The spirit as a meta-rational capacity of our consciousness makes it possible to experience time as a co-creative life process.

THE DEEP TERM

Sustainability is primarily associated with attention to the environment and to the resources of the planet. The connotation of the dimension of time is less explicit and visible in the English word.[1] However, sustainability without a long-term time perspective is an illusion. But does it suffice to define time as a long-term perspective to realise sustainability?[2]

The Greeks used at least two words to speak about time: chronos and kairos, both represented as goddesses.[3] Chronos is the succession of moments in time; kairos is the appropriate time, i.e. the right moment to act. In today's language, chariness is measured and quantifiable time, clock time; Kairos is a subjective and qualitative experience of time; time revealing itself as a gift and a guiding force towards acting at the right moment. Chronos has dominated public life since the modern age, with its passion for mechanical clocks. But kairos has not disappeared completely: in the sphere of entrepreneurship and art we open our mind for the guidance of time as an unfolding process. Business spirituality that cultivates the creation of meaning consciously connects with time as kairos rather than chronos.

If we want to activate time as kairos in the economy, we must have some general understanding of the meaning of time in the economic process. As we know, the value of goods and of labor were not measured by classical economists in money but in units of time (labor time). Added value in their view is created by labor and, in particular, by acting faster and more productively than one's competitors and converting this gain in time into lower costs, more output, and hence greater profit. Time is money. Other economic concepts are also linked to time. Interest, for example, is a payment for postponing the present satisfaction of a need in exchange for greater profit in the future. Analyses of financial and ecological crises invariably point to the dominance of short-term thinking at the expense of long-term results. But in all these reflections, time is conceived as chronos: quantifiable *units of time* measured against the clock. Time is hence divorced from creativity and wed to efficiency.

Adam Smith begins *The Wealth of Nations* with a famous and highly detailed description of his visit to a new pin factory. He is in awe of the efficiency with which the tasks are distributed and timed. The output per hour is a multiple of what it used to be. But Smith also recognizes the dangers of this new numbing and mechanical work. In our post-modern age, assembly-line work has largely given way to a more complex variant, the *rat race*. The greater exposure to that experience, and to its consequences, has led to a greater interest in alternatives, which necessarily presuppose a different perception of time.

The kairos concept offers us the 'opportunity' to link time to deep change, spiritual leadership and discernment, intrinsic motivation, and co-creativity. At first sight, all these new concepts are very fragmented, lacking both consistency and coherence. But an interesting international literature is currently developing on time management in Human Resources. This literature dovetails very well with a broad philosophical current of the 20th century that thrives under the names of 'process philosophy' and 'narrative ethics.' What all these share is the conviction that time is not something we make but, rather, a deep term that unfolds itself in reality and guides us. By focusing on the deep term, measurement and control are finally transcended.

In *Theory U* (2009), Otto Scharmer shows how we can

integrate time as kairos into the economy. *Presencing* is the key word of his theory; it means: *getting in touch with the Source from which the future field emerges; seeing from that Source.* To clarify the process, he quotes the Danish sculptor and business consultant Erik Lemcke, who explains how he works as an artist: "After I have worked on a sculpture for a while, there always comes a moment when things change. When that moment arrives, it is no longer 'just me' who creates something. Then I feel connected to something much deeper and my hands co-create with that power (...) Then I intuitively know what to do. My hands know whether I should add something or chop it off. My hands know how the form should manifest. In a way, with that guidance, creating is easy. In those moments, I am filled with gratitude and humility." (Scharmer, 2009:213.)

The main features of *presencing* or source experience are:

1. The centre of gravity of the artist's perception,
    thinking, and acting shifts from 'I-create' to a
    creative 'non-I' consciousness.
2. The 'non-I' consciousness does not mean that
    there is no self-experience. On the contrary, the
    artist experiences himself as a living expression of
    a higher creative consciousness.
3. The higher consciousness gives direction and
    guidance to actions in its own way.

In this description, the spiritual thought process is structured by three moments that constantly mediate each other: the moment of 'letting go,' the moment of a 'transcending' experience, and the moment of creating something new. Entrepreneurs go through an analogous process when they design a new idea.

Much attention in business ethics is rightly paid to virtues, especially what are called the four cardinal virtues: prudence, justice, courage and temperance. But, in addition to these virtues, Christian ethics distinguishes three theological or divine virtues: faith, hope, and love. Faith focuses our minds, hope our actions, and love our being on what transcends us and yet touches us. In the context of a spiritual business ethics hope deserves a special place. It stimulates the imagination to transcend 'unsolvable problems' by coming at them from a different perspective. "When you have exhausted all possibilities, remember this—you haven't." (Thomas A. Edison). The core of this resilience lies in the inner trust that, even if we fail, our endeavors contribute at a deeper level to a better world. The power of authentic hope gives entrepreneurship a meaning that is more original than success and lifts entrepreneurship above operational and strategic thinking.

THE OTHER SCARCITY

In order to understand the economic relevance of deep-term thinking, it is important to emphasize its link with scarcity and growth. Solving scarcity problems is the goal of economic activity and growth is the modern solution. The ancients philosophers counseled frugality to solve scarcity problems, modern economists use the growth of the GDP. But the assumption that growth solves scarcity is coming under greater and greater scrutiny. Not only because we are plundering the planet and thus undermining our future ability not only to grow but to survive. There is another reason too. Our obsession with growth is creating a new scarcity, which is becoming increasingly visible.

The new scarcity is complex. On the one hand, there is

the scarcity resulting from a restless desire of always more (or never enough), stimulated by the growth economy that needs increasing consumption to sustain the production process. To this end, marketing continuously stimulates our 'mimetic desire.' We are triggered to want what others have. The media creates role models for us to compare ourselves to, always unfavorably. We rarely compare ourselves to those who have less. As a result, the demand for *status goods* is rising sharply. Better cars, furniture, houses, and vacations elevate our social status. But "conspicuous consumption" (Thorstein Veblen) requires a permanent increase in resources, until the limit is reached. What that looks like I hope we will never see.

What we already clearly see today is that the rat race of endless consumption makes impossible the meeting of immaterial needs such as solidarity, inner peace, silence, time for family and friends, connection with nature—in short, the possibility of leading a meaningful life. Our current society of consumption, that is to say, has led us to a twin of scarcity: a new material scarcity, resulting from the desire of always more and a *spiritual scarcity,* a lack of spiritual and relational goods; the latter is becoming more and more visible and dire; not only can it not be solved by the traditional growth of GDP but it is, in fact, *caused* by this obsessive ethos of growth. This is reflected in the paradox that the growth of income beyond a certain ceiling no longer correlates with our experience of happiness.

Easterlin is an economist whose research in the 1970s investigated the relationship between income and happiness (Easterlin R., 1973). He compared countries and found that there was no meaningful correlation between income and happiness. People from the Philippines or Puerto Rico do not appear to be any less happy or unhappy, on average, than their rich US neighbors in America. A second finding was that people's happiness, considered over the course of a lifetime, depends little on their income. Other factors—a good family life, having an interesting and challenging job, being part of a close community, having a healthy body, being able to live according to one's ideals, the feeling of being in control of one's life—are far more important.

If people are unhappy today, it is because they do not score well on some of these parameters. Statistics support this: the number of broken families is increasing; loneliness is widespread; young people are generally pessimistic about their future prospects. These are all factors that greatly reduce the happiness index. It is no wonder that rates of depression and suicide are as high as they are. Why then don't governments pay more attention to the growth of happiness instead of the GDP? Bhutan is one country that is attempting to replace the GDP with a national happiness index (Bhutan 2015). What they measure might lead them to the sort of action that needs to take place on a global scale—a profound *mental and social shift* towards more frugality in our consumption and the transition to an economy of hope.

The new scarcity is not linked to any sort of shortage. Rather, as wealth increases and is distributed unequally, the demand for *status goods* increases at the expense of *relational goods* that become scarcer (Bruni & Zamagni, 2007). The latter are goods or services that promote connection and belonging among people and determine our happiness and spiritual well-being. It makes little difference whether the economy takes the form of a capitalist free market economy or a collective state economy as in China.

Is a modern economy conceivable without the twin obsessions of the rat race and the permanent growth of GDP? On the micro level, many examples already show us how to improve the balance between status and relational goods. This is not simply a matter of two separate categories of goods, the reduced output of one being compensated by the increased production of the other. The distinction between status and relational goods focuses on two fundamentally different ways in which we perceive and give meaning to goods and services by placing them in the larger context of human and environmental development. The distinction reflects the extent to which entrepreneurs and consumers respect the context and symbolism of products, inventions, etc. Respect means both tolerance and also pushing boundaries that open up new possibilities. Henk Opdebeeck, coordinator of the Trends Chair in Economics of Hope (U Antwerp), refers to the many names and forms in which the transition economy of hope is realized:

> Various economic schools and movements worldwide are currently searching for such a new form. An economy of hope is thus given various names. It is not only a responsible economy, but also a social, circular, happiness, meaning and community economy. (Opdebeeck 2020:20).

Some models connect with a religious background. The community economy of the Foccolare movement, for example, draws its inspiration from Christian social teaching. The Ashoka movement and deep ecology have a Buddhist background. Others are driven by a secular spirituality in which collective values of belonging and justice provide direction. Eco-personalism connects to a philosophical tradition that starts from the person as a relational subject. Hope is nobody's monopoly. It is our most precious shared treasure.

It would be a great mistake to think that immaterial needs

—beauty, goodness, truth, peace, spirituality—are exclusively of an abstract order. That mistake would make the separation from the material economy unbridgeable. The needs of the spirit are as basic as those of the body. Both goodness and food make life possible. But the needs of the spirit become corrupted when they are turned into the mimetic desire to equal or surpass the other, or reduced to the preferences of homo economicus, who seeks maximum gain and well-being in everything. The human being is a spiritual being driven by the primal desire to love and to be loved. Love in its most general form is the desire to receive, share, and develop life in connection with others. This desire is present in all life, including non-human life. The economy of hope starts from this primal spiritual longing. From this base we can better order our material and social needs, and orient ourselves towards a future far better than the social, economic, and ecological disaster where mimetic desire and homo economicus have led us.

CONCLUSION

Business spirituality has emerged in the context of the impotence of politics to correct the negative effects of the neoliberal globalization of the world economy. Appeal to long-term thinking has proven to be too abstract and vague to decisively reverse the increasing inequality and ecological plundering. Only a deep crisis and the emergence of a leadership that senses the 'kairos moment' for deep change will be able to unlock the future.

Business spirituality is a method for thinking from the future in a context of great uncertainty. Scharmer calls this method 'presencing the future.' This essay has chosen to call it 'the economy of hope' because hope is essentially trust in the future that has been granted to us. Entrepreneurs in many fields are currently working with or transitioning towards an economy of hope. The names vary, from donut economy to integral ecology, but the underlying force is the power of hope.

NOTES

1. BEYOND THE RHINELAND MODEL

1. The concept of 'U turn' has been coined in 2009 by the German American professor Otto Scharmer as a new way of thinking and working in organisations (Scharmer 2009; see also chapter 5).

2. THE POWER OF HOPE

1. Emma Pleeging & Martijn Burger, Rapport "The Hope Barometer. Hoop & Corona", augustus 2020. https://www.thehopeproject.nl/nl/the-hope-barometer

3. CARE AS HOPE

1. In his award-winning book on Levinas,' *No Future without Small Goodness* (2020), Roger Burggraeve points out some ways in which an ecological philosophy can be developed from Levinas. The question remains whether Levinas would endorse these paths. In my view, the exclusive reference to the human face as the source and measure of meaning makes a genuine eco-philosophy impossible.

4. ECONOMY OF HOPE

1. Title of a column of Thomas Hannes in the Dutch Journal *De Standaard,* August 5th, 2020.

5. SPIRITUALITY AS 3D ETHICS

1. The Dutch word 'duurzaamheid' used as translation for sustainability explicitly refers to the time dimension. 'Duren/duurzaam/duurzaamheid' means 'lasting'. It evokes the idea of an experience of time that overcomes the fleetingness of passing time.
2. For a good introduction in the concept of sustainaibilty and its connections with ethics and spirituality, see Laszlo Zsolnai (ed), The Spiritual

Dimension of Business Ethics and Sustainaibility Management, Springer, London, 2015.
3. Another time concept in Greek philosophy is 'ai'oon', eternal time without beginning or end.

REFERENCES

Arendt Hannah, 1992, *Lectures on Kant's Political Philosophy*, Chicago, The University of Chicago Press.

Bhutan, 2015, *Gross National Happiness Index*, The Center for Bhutan Studies & GNH Research, Thimpu, Bhutan.

Bouckaert, L., 2016, 'Filosoof in het Oerwoud. Schweitzers Cultuurkritiek', in:. Bouckaert, L. (red), *Albert Schweitzer. Leven dat leven wil* (pp. 45-62), Yunus Publishing, Gent.

Bouckaert Luk, 2017, 'Authenticity and Sustainability: the Search for a Reliable Earth Spirituality', in: Ove Jakobsen & Laszlo Zsolnai, *Integral Ecology and Sustainable Business*, Emerald publishing, pp. 3-15.

Bouckaert Luk, 2017, *Kies voor hoop. Hoe spiritualiteit de economie kan veranderen (Choose Hope. How spirituality can transform the economy)*, Garant, Antwerpen.

Bouckaert L. (red), 2017, *Mahatma Gandhi. Spiritualiteit in actie.* Yunus Publishing, Gent.

Bouckaert Luk, 2019, 'Caring for Being and Caring for the Other', in: Ora Setter& Laszlo Zsolnai, *Caring Management in the New Economy. Socially Responsible Behaviour Through Spirituality.* Palgrave studies, Springer, pp.47-61.

Bruni Luigino & Zamagni Stefano, 2007, *Civil economy. Efficiency, Equity, Public Happiness.* New York, New City Press.

Buber Martin, 1937 *I and Thou (Ich und Du, 1923) Translated* from German to English in 1937*by Ronald Gregor Smith.* Edinburgh. T. & T. Clark. *Translated in 1970 by Walter Kaufmann. New York: Charles Scribner's Sons.*

Burggraeve Roger, 2020, *Geen toekomst zonder kleine goedheid (No Future without Small Goodness)*, Halewijn, Antwerpen.

Camus Albert, 1947, *La Peste,* Gallimard, Parijs.

Cobbaut, J. 2020, *De mentale exit richting circulaire economie,* Etion Forum 2020, https://www.etion.be/kennisbank/de-mentale-exit-richting-circu laire-economie

Easterlin Richard, 1973, 'Does money buy happiness?', in: *Public Interest*, nr 30, pp. 3-10.

Eynikel Jochanan, 2020, *Check In. Op zoek naar zin en betekenis in bedrijven,* Lannoo Campus, Tielt.

Fromm Erich, 1968, *The Revolution of Hope, toward a humanized technology,* Harper Collins.

Gandhi Mohandas, 2002, *Essential Writings (selected by John Dear)*.Orbis Books, New York.

Gandhi Mohandas, 1957, *The Story of My Experiments with Truth: An Autobiography*, Boston: Beacon Press.

Havel, Václav, 1990 (1986), *Disturbing the Peace (chapter 5: The politics of Hope)*.

Heidegger Martin, 1927, *Sein und Zeit*, Tübingen, Max Niemeyer Verlag.

Kant Immanuel, 2009 (1790), *Kritiek van het oordeelsvermogen (Critique of Judgment)*, Boom, Amsterdam.

Kierkegaard, S., 1983 (1849), *The Sickness unto Death*. In: Kierkegaard's Writings XIX, Princeton University Press.

Hawken Paul (red.), 2017, *Drawdown. The Most Comprehensive Plan Ever Proposed to Reverse Global Warming*, Penguin Books, New York.

Kumar, S., 2002, *You are, Therefore I Am. A Declaration of Dependence*. Cambridge: UIT Cambridge Ltd.

Levinas Emmanuel, 1961, *Totalité et Infini: Essai sur l'Exteriorité*. Martinus Nijhoff, The Hague.

Levinas Emmanuel, 1974, *Autrement qu'être ou au-delà de l'essence*. Martinus Nijhoff, The Hague.

Macy Joanna & Johnstone Chris, 2012, *Active Hope*, New World Library, Novato, USA.

Mendes-Flor Paul, 1989, *From mysticism to Dialogue. Martin Buber's transformation of German Social Thought*. Wayne State University Press, Detroit.

Mounier Emmanuel, 1962, 'Qu'est-ce que le personnalisme?', in: Mounier, E. *Oeuvres de Mounier*. Tome III. Parijs: Ed. du Seuil.

Noels Jolien, 2020, 'De klimaatneutrale transitie als een hefboom voor een menselijkere economie', in: Streven vrijplaats, *Een economie van de hoop*, Antwerpen: pp. 67-70.

Rediger Jeffrey, 2020, *Cured: The Life-changing Science of Spontaneous Healing*, Flatiron Books, New York. (quoted from Dutch translation: *Spontaan Genezen. Op zoek naar de bron van ons zelfhelend vermogen*, AnkhHermes, Utrecht.)

Opdebeeck Hendrik, 2020, 'Ondernemersinitiatief in transitie als economie van de hoop', in: Streven vrijplaats, *Een economie van de hoop*, Antwerpen, pp. 15-25.

Roy, Christian, 1999, 'Ecological Personalism. The Bordeaux School of Bernard Charbonneau and Jacques Ellul', in: *Ethical Perspectives: is Personalism still alive in Europe?*. 6(1), 21-33.

Scharmer C.Otto, 2009, *Theory U. Leading from the Future as at It Emerges*, Berrett-Koehler publishers, San Francisco.

Schumacher Ernst Friedrich, 1973, *Small is Beautiful. Economics as if people mattered*, London, Blond and Briggs.

Schweitzer, 1987 (1923), *The Philosophy of Civilization*, Prometheus books, New York.

Schweitzer, 1998, *Out of my life and thought: An autobiography*, John Hopkins University Press, Baltimore.

Schweitzer, Albert, 2004 (1936), *Les grands penseurs de l'Inde*. Parijs: Éditions Payot.

Semler Ricardo, 2003, *The Seven-day Weekend. A Better Way to Work in the 21st Century*, Random House, London.

Smith Emily Esfahani, 2017, *The Power of Meaning*, Penguin Random House (quoted from Dutch translation *De kracht van betekenis, Hoe zin te geven aan je leven*. Ten Have, Utrecht).

Spinosa Charles, Flores Fernando & Dreyfus Hubert L., 1997, *Disclosing New Worlds. Entrepreneurship, democratic action and the cultivation of solidarity*. The MIT Press, Cambridge.

Zsolnai Laszlo (ed.), 2003, *Spirituality and Ethics in Management*, Springer, Lodon.

Zsolnai Laszlo (ed.), 2015, *The Spiritual Dimension of Business Ethics and Sustainaibility Management*, Springer, London.

Zucman Gabriel & Saez Emmanuel, 2019, *The Triumph of Injustice: How the Rich Dodge Taxes and How to Make Them Pay*, WW Norton & Co.

The Ecological Person
Disclosing Nature as Thou

Luk Bouckaert

Version 1.0

*

Originally published as
Luk Bouckaert, *Ecopersonalisme: een perspectief*, Halewijn, 2021

Translated from Dutch by Sabine Denis
Re-edited by Mikael Bouckaert

Cover: aquarel Miriam Bouckaert

*

Published by
Yunus Publishing
Bolderberg, 2023

www.yunuspublishing.org

ISBN (printed version): 978-94-926-8922-1
ISBN (epub): 978-94-926-8923-8

D/2023/12.808/1

*

9 789492 689221